Medical Dilemmas

Medical Dilemmas

Margaret O. Hyde &
Elizabeth H. Forsyth, M.D.

G. P. Putnam's Sons   New York

Copyright © 1990 by Margaret O. Hyde and Elizabeth H. Forsyth
All rights reserved. This book, or parts thereof, may not be
reproduced in any form without permission in writing from the publisher.
Published by G. P. Putnam's Sons, a division of
The Putnam & Grosset Group, 200 Madison Avenue, New York, N.Y. 10016.
Published simultaneously in Canada
Designed by Christy Hale
Printed in the United States of America

Library of Congress Cataloging-in-Publication Data
Hyde, Margaret O. (Margaret Oldroyd)
Medical dilemmas / Margaret O. Hyde and Elizabeth H. Forsyth.
p.   cm.   Bibliography: p.   Includes index.
Summary: Presents ethical and moral dilemmas relating to
animal research, gene therapy, transplants, AIDS,
mercy killing, and other controversial medical areas.
1. Medical innovations—Moral and ethical aspects
—Juvenile literature. 2. Medical ethics—Juvenile
literature. [1. Medical innovations—Moral and
ethical aspects. 2. Medical ethics.]
I. Forsyth, Elizabeth Held. II. Title.
R855.4.H83 1990   174'.2—dc20   89–34985   CIP   AC
ISBN 0–399–21902–1

1   3   5   7   9   10   8   6   4   2

The policy statement of the American Humane Association which
appears on pages 22 through 24 is quoted with permission.

To Edwin Y. Hyde and Ben R. Forsyth, M.D.

Contents

1

Matters of Life
and Death

Many wonderful medical technologies have been developed in recent years, but enthusiasm about them is tempered by ethical and moral issues. There are agonizing questions for doctors, lawyers, patients and their families, and the public in general, as doctors apply new ways of healing and prolonging life. Choices are made each day about situations for which there are no right or wrong answers, and many of these choices pertain to matters of life and death. Although each case is different, the search for guidelines has become increasingly important.

Suppose a letter in today's mail asks you to give the gift of life to a dying child. All you have to do is sign a card specifying that your organs be donated for transplantation at the time of your death. No one promises that they will go to the dying child described in the brochure, but you can hope that they will save a life when yours is gone. Few people question the great need for organs for transplants and the value of signing a donor card. But there are questions to be asked about how these organs are used.

If, for example, two children need heart transplants and only one suitable organ is available, which child should be chosen? Or suppose a young boy needs a fourth liver transplant. He has little chance of surviving, since this time may not be more successful than the others. Should this child be eligible for still another transplant? When should doctors decide to make scarce organs and other hospital facilities available to people who have a better chance of survival? Is it fair to spend so much time and money on a child who has little chance of survival? Could you be objective if you were the boy's doctor or his parent?

Even thornier questions arise when organs are taken from fetal tissue. In the case of the first fetal-cell transplant that took place in Mexico, tissue was taken from a fetus that had been spontaneously aborted when a thirty-one-year-old woman suffered a miscarriage after thirteen weeks of pregnancy. The woman gave permission to use brain tissue from the fetus in experimental transplants into the brains of two people who suffered from Parkinson's disease, a progressive nerve disorder that causes hand and head tremors, muscle rigidity, and many other problems. The woman who miscarried was not related to either recipient, so no one could say she became pregnant just to abort the fetus and supply tissue for the recipients. However, many objections were voiced because of this experimental operation. In fact, the whole subject of fetal-cell surgery raises much controversy.

Suppose a woman becomes pregnant just to have an abortion and provide tissue for a loved one. Or imagine if women were pressured to become fetal factories because they needed money and hoped to sell fetal tissue on the black market. These are two of the worst possible scenarios.

Fetal tissue is especially valuable for transplants since it will not be rejected by its new host the way adult tissue is. When transplanted, fetal brain cells readily form connections throughout the central nervous system. Fetal tissue continues to produce chemicals that are missing from the bodies of the diseased recipients into whom it is transplanted. Although early results have been disappointing, doctors hope that fetal tissue may someday help people who suffer from Alzheimer's disease, a major illness involving memory loss, personality changes, and other serious disorders, or from vision and hearing defects, diabetes, brain damage, and a variety of other problems.

While the use of fetal tissues obtained from miscarriages remains controversial, there is little disagreement that the science itself is promising. In Britain, a doctor who performed fetal-cell surgery on two patients suffering from Parkinson's disease said, in response to criticism, that it was erroneous to suggest that the way is being opened up for the production of embryos for spare-part surgery. Many doctors feel that so many people could be helped by fetal-cell surgery that it would be immoral not to proceed, as long as strict guidelines were followed.

Obtaining informed consent for controversial treatments can be another problem for which there are no clear answers. Mrs. Jones has been suffering from Alzheimer's disease for many years. A new drug might help to improve her condition, which is hopelessly pathetic and getting worse. Her husband is worn out from caring for her. As her doctor, you want to try the experimental drug, but you need consent before you can prescribe it for your patient. Who can give informed consent? Certainly not Mrs. Jones. Her husband is willing to give her the drug, but her son fears this might be dangerous. The young man claims that his father is willing to submit her to the experiment because he is tired of caring for her. As her doctor, you have seen the husband's devotion, and you know that the son is wrong. Should you proceed without the son's consent, since you can legally do so?

Alice is only twenty years old, but she wants to be allowed to die. She has been living without the use of her arms and legs for seven years. She knows she is a burden to her family and she no longer enjoys any part of her life. Does she have a right to refuse food?

These are just a few examples of cases in which there are no easy answers. Who should make decisions in matters of life and death? You may need to make difficult choices about something in your own life or the lives of family members or someone you know, now or in the future.

Advances in medical technology bring questions about high-tech babies; about gene implantation to treat certain diseases, and other experiments on human beings; about the use of animals for medical experiments; about the right to die and even the very definition of death. As medicine becomes more sophisticated, each person needs information about the controversies that can arise and the many factors involved in making wise decisions. Everyone should know about the legal and moral dilemmas created by recent medical advances.

Even the differences between right and wrong come into the picture. When one is talking about severe physical abuse of a six-year-old, the answers are easy, for everyone considers child abuse wrong. But what about the boy who needed another liver transplant? What seems right to one person may be very different from what seems right to another. In a fable by Leo Tolstoy, "Why There Is Evil in the World," the dove that is eaten has fallen on evil times, while the person or animal who eats the dove has fallen on good times. This illustrates the point that what is evil for one creature is not necessarily evil for another.

When a badly deformed baby needs an operation in order to prevent its death, who should make the decision, and on

what factors should that decision be based? Should the feelings of parents be considered? Should they have the final
word in a decision? Should society be willing to spend more
money to treat babies who suffer from fetal alcohol syndrome, a tragic condition caused by the mother's excessive
drinking during pregnancy, than to educate pregnant women
about the dangers of drinking?

Suppose a man who has been imprisoned for murder
needs a bone marrow transplant. In most cases, prisoners are
transferred to a medical center for care and then returned to
jail. However, surgery for a bone marrow transplant costs
over $100,000, and prison officials cannot allocate this
amount of money for the operation. If the prisoner is given
early parole, the money for his operation would come from
public funds. Is it fair for the state to pay for the prisoner's
operation when other individuals who need bone marrow
transplants have to pay for their own? Does the prisoner de-
serve equal access to medical care?

These are just a few of the many questions that are difficult to answer in today's world, in which a balance between
moral and technical orders is being sought. Decisions of life
and death are far more difficult than and very different from
those of past times, when nature played the major role. Life
support systems can sustain lives most people do not consider worth living. In the past, doctors were accused of playing God; today, in an increasing number of cases,
individuals from many walks of life are involved in making
ethical decisions. The following chapters may help you make
wise choices in matters involving life and death.

2

Animals for Medical Research

The controversy over the use of animals for research has grown dramatically in the last 15 years. In the early 1970s, animal welfare advocates were largely confined to people who belonged to humane societies, but today much of the debate has spread to the general public and it has become heated and emotional. The number of animal protection groups had grown to about 7,000 in 1989.

Many people see the problem of animals rights only in black and white, sometimes for entirely different reasons. The use of animals for laboratory research touches a raw nerve in many compassionate people who unconsciously empathize with all helpless creatures. On the other hand, there are people who feel that overpopulation of the earth by humans has upset the balance of nature so greatly that they should volunteer for experiments that benefit their own species. Medical researchers vary from feelings that practical benefits for mankind justify any experiment on any kind of animal to conscientious efforts to use alternatives to animal experimentation.

While some people believe strongly in one idea or another, many are finding a middle ground. The moderate groups advocate the "three R's" which are: the reduction of the number of animals sacrificed, the refinement of techniques that cause suffering, and the replacement of live animals with simulations or cell cultures. Advanced technologies, such as computer, mathematical, and mechanical models are used to simulate many systems of the human body. Artificial membranes, robots, and chemical systems serve as alternatives in an increasing number of experiments. While progress is being made in the use of viable alternatives for animals in many kinds of research, doctors point out that alternatives are not always available. Some complex biological systems cannot be easily duplicated.

Some animal welfare organizations tolerate experiments in which animals do not suffer; others evaluate the use of animals in experimental research on the basis of how much it will help humans. These groups do not believe animals should be made to suffer in order to produce a better lipstick, but they approve of the use of animals for medical research when there is no alternative.

Scientists feel that there is a tremendous gulf between activities on the forefront of research and understanding by the general public. They say many people do not consider the comparative value of their work. Is Professor David J. Edell of the Harvard-MIT Division of Health Sciences and Technology treating rabbits cruelly when he injects microelectrodes into the spinal cords of anesthetized rabbits? His work could result in an implant that would use signals from a human's spinal cord to control a paralyzed body. Is the welfare of people paralyzed by spinal cord injuries more important than the welfare of the rabbits? What about the blinding of cats in efforts to learn more about human blindness? Should such experiments be stopped until alternative methods are found?

Some members of animal rights groups believe that every insect, every snake, and every mouse have as much right to life as a human. But for many activists, the use of mice in experiments is more acceptable than the use of cats, dogs, and monkeys. Of the approximately 17 million animals that are used in laboratory experiments each year, about 85 percent are rats and mice. Although the need for some experiments may be controversial, many of the thousands of cats, dogs, rabbits, and primates used in experiments have helped to save human lives, lessen human suffering, and advance scientific understanding, according to medical researchers.

Pressure from animal rights advocates has changed the way some scientists are experimenting and has even brought about the end of some research. For example, Dr. Michiko Okamoto, a scientist at Cornell Medical College, received many complaints from animal rights activists about her experiments which used cats to test drug addiction. In November of 1988, Dr. Okamoto abandoned her study and began a new project in which she uses rats to study alcohol addiction. The protests stopped, perhaps because these animals are less appealing.

Although some groups want a moratorium on approving patents for new kinds of animals so that the economic and moral issues can be studied more carefully, the United States Patent and Trademark Office issued the first patent for a high form of life on April 13, 1988. This transgenic (an animal produced with genes from two animals) was a mouse created by scientists at Harvard Medical School in an effort to hasten the development of treatment for cancer in humans. Many people ask, "How can anybody say this kind of development is unethical or wrong?" However, others believe that such "tampering with living things" is wrong.

There is little disagreement that genetically altered mice

can serve as more effective models for studying how genes contribute to the development of cancer and other diseases. In the fall of 1988, researchers at Stanford University reported separately that they had transplanted elements of the human immune system into mice, making a strain of mice that was later infected with the AIDS virus. This was another step forward in altering mice so they can be stand-ins for studying of human diseases and vaccines and for testing of new drugs and therapies. They may also help in determining which substances in food and the environment are harmful, and this may lead to developments in medicine, forestry, agriculture, and a variety of industries.

While some people hail the news of progress with genetically engineered laboratory animals, not everyone is enthusiastic. "Will this lead to more testing in which animals suffer unnecessarily?" is a question asked by animal rights activists who are still working to eliminate cruel laboratory tests introduced years ago.

One of the procedures that has raised a great deal of furor is the Draize eye-irritation test, which is used to measure the safety of cosmetics and other consumer products. In the spring of 1933, when a woman known only as Mrs. Brown applied mascara to her eyelashes, some of the dye got into her eyes. Not only did she suffer constant pain for three months, but she lost her sight. Her case played an important part in the passage of the Food, Drug and Cosmetic Act of 1938, which gave the federal Food and Drug Administration the power to prohibit the sale of harmful cosmetics.

Following the passage of the Food, Drug and Cosmetic Act, tests were developed to evaluate the safety of cosmetics. Manufacturers needed animals on which to test their products, and rabbits were chosen for many experiments. Each year, about 100,000 rabbits were removed from their laboratory cages and restrained while their eyes were squirted with measured doses of suspected irritants. Over the course of a few days, their eyes were examined to see if they were red, blistered, or bleeding. In some cases the rabbits became blind.

In recent years, ways of testing for skin and eye safety using fewer or even no animals have been introduced. Researchers at a number of universities and medical schools have developed batteries of tests that measure the safety of cosmetics and other products in cell cultures. One animal usually provides enough tissue for numerous samples. In some cases the tissue can be propagated indefinitely, serving study after study.

In the case of the Draize test, the credit for some of the changes in testing goes to animal rights activists. Henry Spira, a leading activist in the movement, was instrumental in saving the eyes of huge numbers of rabbits through innovative and nonviolent actions. In one of his dramatic efforts, he organized a protest in 1980 against the cosmetic manufacturer Revlon. He and his supporters ran full-page ads in newspapers showing bandaged white rabbits with the caption; "How many rabbits does Revlon blind for beauty's sake?" Some of his supporters donned rabbit costumes and paraded in front of the Revlon corporate offices. Today, some alternatives to the Draize test are in limited use and a number of new tests are being developed. Eventually this test may be replaced entirely by methods involving the use of chicken eggs or cell cultures taken from a variety of sources.

While some protests about the use of animals in research have helped make researchers aware that there can be better ways to test the safety of new household cleansers, radiator fluids, shampoos, and cosmetics, a small percentage of animal rights activists have carried their cause into the realm of terrorism. By early 1988, the Federal Bureau of Investigation had begun to investigate several arson cases involving research laboratories and meat companies where animals had been cruelly slaughtered. Research projects have been set back years by raids on laboratories where animals are kept for experimental purposes.

One example of the destruction of years of hard work took place in the summer of 1987, when a group known as the Band of Mercy cut a chain-link fence at the U.S. Department of Agriculture's Animal Parasitology Institute in Beltsville, Maryland. Members of the group, thinking they were rescuing cats from cruel experiments, made off with the animals in backpacks. In addition to rescuing the cats, they felt that the publicity about their actions would further the cause of animal rights. However, eleven of the stolen cats were infected with the parasite *Toxoplasma gondii,* which can cause birth defects and other problems in humans under certain conditions, and some of the liberated cats may have spread infection to other cats and to people.

About 40 percent of the cats in the United States carry the parasite that was being studied in the laboratory. Although it rarely causes symptoms in cats, if a pregnant woman becomes infected by inadvertently ingesting the egglike form of the parasite, her baby may be born with visual problems or suffer mental retardation. Each year, an estimated 2,000 birth defects in the United States are attributed to toxoplasmosis. The disease is also a threat to people with damaged immune systems, such as people with AIDS.

How do people become infected? They may be gardening in soil where a cat has defecated and then forget to wash their hands before they handle food. Or they may change cat litter and then work in the kitchen before washing their hands. Contaminated food thereby enters the digestive system.

Even though many cats are infected, only about 1 percent of them at any one time shed the egglike form of the parasite that causes the trouble. Researchers studying the liberated cats tried to learn more about how the disease is spread, whether cats pass the disease to their offspring, and the answers to other questions.

Even though just about every surgical technique and every drug used in medicine today was tried first on animals, an increasing number of individuals resort to violence that could kill humans in their effort to defend lower animals. Raids, bomb threats, and fires are used in attempts to save animals from what activists consider unnecessary cruelty. In November of 1988, after a 33-year-old dog lover attempted to bomb the headquarters of the United States Surgical Company in Norwalk, Connecticut, where trainees practice stapling multiple incisions on anesthetized dogs, activist groups quickly disavowed the use of violence, saying that it was damaging to their cause.

The need for using large numbers of animals to test drugs and other chemicals that may be toxic to humans has been brought into question. An estimated 1,000 new chemicals enter the market each year. Many of these are not tested at all, but the comparatively few commercially important chemicals that are tested involve an estimated 14 million animals each year. Many of these tests cost thousands of dollars and may take as long as two years. Some are of dubious value because drugs that are harmful to humans may not be harmful to laboratory animals. Conversely, some drugs that are harmful to animals may not be harmful to humans, so new drugs that may be valuable to humans are screened out through the toxicity tests. Scientists who are exploring alternatives to animal testing suggest that the time has come to reevaluate current practices. Many animal tests are outdated and unsophisticated.

One of the most common and controversial measures used in testing the effects of various substances on animals is known as the LD50 test. This test determines the minimum dose of a substance that kills half of the test animals. Large numbers of animals are used in order to arrive at a precise figure, but this information must then be applied to humans. Calculated values vary from laboratory to laboratory and from one species of animal to another. Because they vary so much, the test is being modified and a number of alternatives have been developed that reduce the number of animals needed. In some cases, in vitro testing (testing outside living animals) is used, but in other cases, animal tests are more accurate.

Although there are safeguards in effect that protect animals from abuse, some cases of maltreatment and unnecessary cruelty do exist. Researchers insist that such cases are rare. They point out that animals must be treated humanely since research depends on using clean, healthy subjects not under emotional and physical stress. Scientists feel increased regulations for the protection of animals inhibit research. Suppose a researcher has permission to pursue a specified experiment, but in the middle of it an opportunity arises to learn about something different. Must the scientist wait for ethics committee approval of the project? Might he or she be discouraged from pursuing it because of red tape?

Many activists who are not well informed often appeal to the emotions of pet lovers in their efforts to stop the use of animals in medical research. Even the activists themselves may be unaware that about 90 percent of the animals are mice, rats, and other rodents. To some the pain of animals seems more important than the pain of people. They do not realize that animals too have profited from research on animal models that has resulted in treatment and cures for human diseases. Many family pets have undergone heart surgery, wear pacemakers, and have had cataracts removed. Vaccines protect them from disease. Many pet owners would even be willing to sacrifice their own animals for the sake of research that would save human lives.

Animals rights groups such as the Humane Society of the United States agree that some animal research is necessary for the discovery of lifesaving scientific advances, but they work toward the replacement, reduction, and refinement of animal experiments. While cell culture experiments and computer models can help in this direction, how can researchers test new kinds of surgery, learn about treatments for bone diseases, and practice other techniques without the use of animal models? Legislation that severely restricts animal research has been introduced at local, state, and federal levels. According to the Foundation for Biomedical Research, a nationwide survey indicates that 77 percent of the American people support the use of animals in biomedical research; but the issue continues to be highly emotional and controversial.

While most people are for the necessary use of animals in medical research since they serve as surrogates in investigations that require biological systems, they plead for the most humane care and treatment of animal research subjects. The following statement expresses the position of the American Humane Association in regard to the use of animals in research:

The Use of Animals in Research

The American Humane Association does not seek

to abolish any specific use of animals by and for the betterment of mankind or other animals, but solely to prevent cruelty or mistreatment. American Humane urges that the models or species of animals to be used be selected on the basis of sound scientific and economic reasons and that the experiments will provide data unavailable elsewhere. American Humane abhors the indiscriminate selection of a particular animal species on the basis of a "fad" or "in" species at any given time. This is unscientific and creates a needless waste of precious animal life as well as the likelihood of publishing questionable data.

American Humane suggests as a general principle that nonhuman primates should be used only when their characteristics are vital to the research effort.

Recognizing that all animals used in biomedical research have social instincts and emotional needs, American Humane urges all concerned with the care, treatment and research effort of animals to practice compassion, a deep feeling for and understanding of misery or suffering and the concomitant desire to promote its alleviation.

American Humane continues to support the Federal Animal Welfare Acts as they relate to research animals and their enforcement and any necessary future legislation that will insure stricter standards for the care, management and use of animals in medical research.

Monitoring and the enforcement of the Animal Welfare Act regulations [are] major problem[s]. Investigations by private organizations have shown that cruelty and abuse [continue] in an uncontrolled state at various research institutions.

American Humane calls for proper screening of research proposals to assure that the experimental activity is not duplication, thus causing the suffering of more animals for data already available.

According to the Foundation for Biomedical Research, pound animals contribute much to the progress of biomedical studies. An estimated 12 million unwanted animals are killed in pounds or shelters in the United States each year, and fewer than 200,000 of them are released to researchers, but there is much concern about the possible use of lost pets.

Animals in pounds are held for a waiting period so that any that are not strays may be claimed by their owners. Most animals that are not claimed are put to death. Scientists purchase about 2 percent of the animals for medical research before they are destroyed. Since some of these animals will experience pain during the experiments, a number of animal rights activists are opposed to the use of pound animals for research. If they were turned loose, some of the animals might be adopted. Another reason these activists object to using pound animals is that the availability of cheap animals for laboratory research does not encourage alternatives to animal testing. In addition, animal rights supporters feel that pound animals do not make reliable research subjects because their backgrounds are unknown, and thus it is difficult to obtain accurate drug evaluations and other research information. Do you agree with these reasons? Or do you agree with those who feel that if pound animals were not available, there would be more dognapping by people who sell pets to research laboratories?

Groups in favor of humanely conducted animal research suggest that those who oppose the use of all animals consider a possibility like the following: You are told that you must undergo serious surgery. The doctor asks for your permission to try a new procedure that he feels is the only approach to saving your life. He has been prevented from trying it on a research animal. At this point, would you wish that the surgeon had been able to try the new procedure on a lower form of animal life?

Do you agree with Dr. Lewis P. Lipsitt, editor of the *Brown University Child Behavior and Development Letter*, who says that interfering with respectable, humanely conducted animal research is as unconscionable as killing a ten-year-old child to save a rat, rabbit, or monkey?

The heightened controversy over animal rights and the need for animals in research led to a study by the National Research Council of the National Academy of Sciences. A report of this group released in September 1988 noted that "research with animals has saved human lives, lessened human suffering, and advanced scientific understanding." The report said that in the best judgment of people with diverse opinions, it is appropriate to use animals in research for human welfare despite the pain suffered by the animals. One member of the panel refused to sign the report, however, because she believed it underestimated the amount of animal abuse in laboratories throughout the United States. Some members of animal rights groups said that the report was flawed because it was paid for by the National Institutes of Health and by pharmaceutical companies that use animals in research. So the controversy continues.

3

Gene Therapy

"Help my child," pleads Mrs. Jones, who is attending a special meeting of an ethics committee, a group who considers the medical and moral aspects of controversial cases. They have been called to discuss the possibility of relieving the symptoms of an unusual disease by the experimental method known as gene therapy. The patient is a ten-year-old boy named Tom, who suffers from Lesch-Nyhan syndrome, a rare form of cerebral palsy. His hands are strapped to his wheelchair in the daytime and to the sides of his crib at night. He has uncontrollable urges to chew on his fingers and arms, and he might even amputate a finger by biting hard if he were not restrained. His teeth have been removed so that he will not bite his lips and his tongue.

Tom lives in a body racked with palsy, his mind driven with compulsions to destroy part of his own body. His mother says he is aware of his self-destructive behavior but he cannot stop it. Although he usually has a good sense of humor, Tom may suddenly spit food at someone or behave in another bizarre way. Experimental drugs have given only short relief, and the periodic uncontrollable urges continue.

Mrs. Jones is begging the ethics committee to approve the radical new gene therapy.

Tom's condition is the result of a defect in a single gene in each of the 100 trillion cells in his body. This defective gene, one of about 100,000 that are present in each cell, is responsible for the lack of an enzyme known as hypoxanthine-guanine phosphoribosyl transferase (HPRT), an enzyme needed to break down certain compounds. When HPRT is lacking, there is a buildup of uric acid, a compound normally present in the urine of humans in very small amounts. Excessive uric acid can cause gout and severe kidney damage, but it can be controlled to some degree by medication. In addition to the uric-acid waste buildup in Lesch-Nyhan syndrome, the lack of HPRT produces bizarre symptoms such as the compulsive urges toward self-mutilation mentioned earlier.

Gene therapy may someday dramatically change the lives of many people, for when it works it will be a cure for diseases that are presently incurable. Sufferers have long been treatable by surgery to correct malformations, and by diet and/or medication, but these treatments only lessen the symptoms of their diseases. By 1990, gene therapy efforts exploded across the pages of scientific journals, and there were predictions that it would cause a medical revolution as far-reaching as that resulting from the development of antibiotics. Several years after national guidelines were approved for gene therapy to be used against a range of fatal hereditary diseases, doctors are still trying to solve important problems before proceeding. They want to make certain there is more chance of success than in the first known attempts, made in 1970 and 1980 without federal approval. Much more is known about gene therapy today, but caution remains.

Genes are the blueprints that cells use to make proteins for the many functions of the body. They are somewhat like beads on the chromosomes in each of the trillions of cells in the human body. These chromosomes are constructed from DNA (deoxyribonucleic acid), a molecule that has been studied extensively. Although it is impossible to imagine the complexity of the genetic code recorded in the chemical structure of DNA, it helps if one considers that the DNA coiled inside just one living cell would be six to seven feet long if it were stretched out. The information encoded in each cell's DNA is estimated to be as much as that in 10,000 books.

One approach to learning more about genes is by making a complete map of their location in each cell; this gigantic task is under way at the present time. Another approach is changing DNA by snipping a gene out of a molecule of DNA and putting it somewhere else. This is done by inserting the material into a harmless virus or into bacteria that can invade the cells of the desired organism. Instructions for the basic chemistry of life are encoded in genes, and numerous faulty genes have already been recognized and located. The replacement of faulty genes that cause disease is one of the promises of gene therapy.

Thousands of different diseases are caused by gene disorders, and an estimated 10 percent of people carry a gene for a potentially handicapping abnormality. Defective or missing genes account for 30 percent of pediatric admissions to major hospitals. The consequences of inherited disorders range from serious ones such as Lesch-Nyhan syndrome and tendencies toward cancer and heart disease, to mild ones such as nearsightedness and color blindness.

Many inherited diseases involve just a single gene, others involve a number of genes, and still others involve a combination of multiple genes and environmental factors. There are about 3,000 disorders that involve only a single gene, and some of these are the early targets of the gene doctors.

Two diseases are special candidates for gene therapy. One is a rare inherited disease known as adenosine deaminase deficiency (ADA). David, the famous boy who spent most of his life in a germ-free plastic bubble before he died at the age of twelve, suffered from ADA. In 1984 he received a bone marrow transplant with the hope that it would enable him to live a more normal life, but cells from the donated marrow attacked his body instead of boosting his immune system. People across the country, who knew him only as David, mourned his death.

Since the time of David's death, not only has the defective gene for ADA been isolated, but normal copies of it have been grown in the laboratory. The same is true for the gene that is responsible for Lesch-Nyhan syndrome.

Suppose Tom's case were approved for an experimental procedure. After applying local anesthesia, a doctor would insert a hypodermic needle into his hipbone until it hit the marrow, the spongy matter that fills the bone's cavity. About a tablespoonful of cells would be withdrawn and taken to the hospital laboratory. Here the cells would be incubated with viruses redesigned to carry the normal gene and replace his disabled one. Doctors would hope that when the marrow cells were infused into Tom's bloodstream later in the day, they would reach his bone marrow, and cells with the normal gene would be reproduced to direct the production of the enzyme that his body lacks. It might be weeks, or even months, before any results could be seen, but if the procedure worked, cells with the normal gene would be reproduced and would churn out the enzyme missing from his body. After a number of infusions into his bone marrow, many of his symptoms might gradually disappear.

Although Tom's mother is eager for such an operation to proceed, she has little idea of the complexity of the problem, even though the doctor has tried to explain it to her. Doctors who have been studying Lesch-Nyhan syndrome for many years are concerned whether or not treating the genetic defect in the bone marrow will clear up the problems that involve the central nervous system. No one knows how to get the virus that carries the corrected gene into the brain.

Although many individuals will probably benefit from gene therapy after it is no longer an experimental procedure, it is not expected to be a panacea. An increasing number of people with different diseases will be able to live normal lives with regular infusions of bacteria or viruses that are engineered to produce the normal genes in their bodies, but much remains to be learned.

The idea of replacing defective genes in living cells is one that provokes much emotional debate. When the technique of gene splicing was invented in the 1970s, many people expressed fear that the creation of new life forms might result in the escape from the laboratory of a microbe that could kill vast numbers of people who had no natural protection from it. Visions of strange diseases, monsterlike animals, and runaway experiments provoked fear and sharp controversy about replacing genes in many kinds of plants and animals. The questions are still being asked: Should humans be allowed to tamper with nature? Should scientists be allowed to redesign existing organisms even if it means the elimination of diseases?

Many new life forms have appeared because of mutations, changes in genes. Numerous new botanical life forms—such as tangelos, various colored flowers, and crops that are disease-resistant and have higher yields—have long been accepted even though their heredity has been altered by humans through breeding. Selective breeding has been used with animals for many years. But the insertion of genes into animals and plants in efforts to produce desired traits and correct undesirable ones is a relatively new science.

In at least one case, concern about harmful effects delayed the release of genetically altered bacteria into the atmosphere for three years. Known as Frostban, the altered bacteria lacked the gene that allows frost to develop. They replaced some of the bacteria that naturally cover strawberry plants and promote the formation of ice crystals of exposed surfaces, destroying the yield. There were fears that the altered bacteria might cause disease in plants, threaten human health, or spread beyond the test area, but none of these things happened.

The list of new drugs that are being developed through genetic engineering is growing. Pharmaceutical companies have products in clinical testing or on the market that are used for anemia, heart attacks, cancer, AIDS, hemophilia, heart failure, burns, skin wounds, and other problems. The arrival of many new drugs signals the transition of genetic engineering from the laboratory to the marketplace, and in this area there is less controversy than in many others.

Genetic engineering is reasonably well accepted in the plant world too. Plant breeders can produce new strains in a matter of months instead of years. But when higher animals become involved, the "slippery slope" argument arises. In other words, how far will scientists go in their efforts to produce desirable traits and correct defects once they begin?

Animal scientists are producing new species of animals known as transgenics through the transfer of genes from one kind of animal to another. Critics feel that this is a violation of animal rights, while advocates point out that the natural transfer of genes between species has gone on throughout evolution.

In 1983 geneticists succeeded in producing mice that grew to be twice their normal size, by injecting a gene for rat growth hormone into fertilized mice ova, or eggs. Since then, more than 100 types of mice with genes from other species have been created in laboratories. Some of the animals did not grow well and had health defects, but the genes were successfully incorporated in their bodies. In some cases the new genes were passed on to the second and third generations.

Pigs with genes from cows have been produced at the United States Department of Agriculture Hawkes Laboratory for over four years. The pigs, which have been injected with the growth genes of cows, produce the same meat as normal pigs, but they eat 20 percent less and their meat contains 20 percent less fat. This sounds wonderful to farmers and nutritionists, but the pigs are not without health problems such as arthritis. Geeps, combinations of sheep and goats, are little more than a scientific curiosity. As research progresses, however, many questions are still being asked about the ethics of manipulating genes. Many people call for strict lines to be drawn governing the appropriate use of genetic engineering on humans.

Those who look to the future predict the following: routine transplants of genes from one species to another; the insertion of genes into plants by way of bacteria, to enable them to produce their own fertilizers and pesticides; the manipulation of sperm and egg cells to enable breeders to select the characteristics they seek in farm animals; and more. When it comes to inserting genes in humans to replace defective genes, scientists have proceeded with great caution as they work toward changing the basic programming present in human cells.

Most ethicists are in favor of using gene therapy to repair defects that cause severe illness. If you had the power to approve a treatment that could relieve the suffering of a child with Lesch-Nyhan syndrome, what would you do?

In rare instances, children are born with a condition known as pituitary dwarfism; they lack some of the hormone needed for normal growth. They can grow to normal height if they are given more growth hormone. Natural hormone must be harvested from cadavers, and it used to take from 50 to 100 cadavers to supply enough for one child. Treatments cost about $10,000 per year and had to be continued for as long as ten years. Today synthetic hormone is available on a much larger scale, now that human growth hormone genes have been inserted into microbes and farmed in laboratories to yield a product that is very nearly the same as the natural one.

Humulin, for the treatment of diabetes, was the first drug to be churned out by large numbers of bacteria with human genes installed in them. It is superior to insulin taken from animals in a number of ways. In the cases of both Humulin and growth hormone, genetically engineered hormones modify the body by adding to the natural supplies. They alter the body without the direct insertion of genes into the cells of the body.

While the fear of tampering with the basic chemicals of life is less common today, since the introduction of drugs produced through genetic engineering, many questions remain about replacing genes directly in humans who suffer from inherited diseases.

In gene therapy for diseases mentioned in this chapter, the

treatment does not involve genes that would be carried from one generation to the next. Genes inserted into the body of a person with a hereditary disease would not be inserted into the reproductive cells. Many scientists and ethicists draw the line at tampering with genes in egg and sperm cells that would pass the altered characteristics of humans from one generation to the next.

Not everyone agrees that it would be wrong to correct genetic disorders in such a way that succeeding generations would be affected. Whether or not any kind of gene therapy is considered ethical often depends on an individual's involvement with someone who is suffering from an inherited disease. Whenever the chance of finding answers to some of the mysteries of the many diseases grouped as cancer is recognized, support for genetic research and gene therapy increases greatly.

Gene therapy for relieving gene disorders is far more widely accepted than genetic manipulation to "improve" normal individuals by making them taller, stronger, or more intelligent. Biologists have come a long way in learning to alter genes. As they move into the brave new world of gene therapy, medical controversy will continue. While critics complain that scientists are reducing life to the status of manufactured commodities, others see the use of the new knowledge as an exaltation of human possibilities.

In working toward correcting defective genes, scientists can learn more about the causes of many kinds of diseases and why some treatments that do not involve gene therapy work. For instance, when scientists were first given permission to insert foreign genes into humans, the experiment was aimed at helping doctors monitor the effectiveness of a kind of cancer treatment. Early in 1989, the National Institutes of Health approved the insertion of bacterial genes into disease-fighting white blood cells that were taken from cancer patients and then returned to them. The altered cells can act as markers, making it possible for researchers to check tumor samples for their presence.

The approval for transplanting foreign genes into humans was granted for experiments in only ten cancer patients who were not expected to live more than 90 days. These patients were informed that the experiment would not help them. However, they signed consent forms for they knew that the purpose of the experiment was to help doctors monitor the effectiveness of cancer treatment that could help others. The successful transplantation of the genes marked with the bacteria could also help scientists to find out how well human genes function after they are transplanted. Although splicing, analyzing, and rebuilding genes have now become routine, proving the effectiveness and safety of gene transfer is a major step toward gene therapy.

Suppose you become involved in a survey on how the public feels about certain forms of gene therapy. You have been to a lecture about the risks of genetic engineering, in which the speaker accused scientists of treating animals as merely assemblies of genes that can be manipulated at will by humans. He pleads for the end of all research that involves genetic engineering. Then you read about some new research in which scientists discovered the protein whose absence triggers the onset of Duchenne muscular dystrophy. Boys who have this disease rarely live beyond their early twenties and suffer severely from muscular weakness. Researchers have been trying to determine the cause of the disease for 130 years, but just five months after the discovery of the muscular dystrophy gene, they discovered a protein that may be missing in people with Duchenne muscular dystrophy. Its absence may be the first of a cascade of events that lead to muscle weakness. Genetic engineering made this discovery possible, and through it doctors may someday be able to treat the disease. With the remarks of the lecturer and the information from the article fresh in your mind, how would you answer a questionnaire that includes a vote for or against genetic research?

4

Difficult Decisions About Babies

A newborn who is suffering from convulsions is rushed from the birthing room to the intensive care unit of the largest hospital in the city. A neonatologist, a doctor who specializes in the care of premature and severely ill infants, immediately prescribes a drug that quiets the convulsions. When she examines the tiny boy she finds that he seems normal except for the size of his head, which is quite small. Further tests show that much of the baby's brain is missing and that the small amount that is present is grossly abnormal. The doctor has the difficult task of telling the parents that their baby has a severe brain defect. They are bewildered and wonder what they have done to cause such a condition. She has no answer to give them other than that it is unlikely the cause was anything over which they had any control. The doctor knows that the baby will never be able to smile at them, to know them as mother and father, to enjoy their love for him. He will never have any knowledge of the world about him or achieve any of the interpersonal relationships that are considered human. He does appear to experience pain. Together, the parents and the doctor discuss the baby's future.

The year is 1981. At this time, the decision is a private

matter between the doctor and the parents. One possible approach is to continue the use of the drug that was introduced to stop the convulsions. If the baby continues to receive the drug, he will not be able to suck and swallow or breathe on his own, so he will spend his life on a mechanical respirator in the hospital. The parents, after questioning what kind of life this would be, decide that keeping the baby attached to tubes and on a mechanical respirator would only prolong the suffering of a child who has no hope of a meaningful life. They ask the doctor to discontinue the drug so that he will be able to take nourishment from his mother's breasts. Now they can take him home, where he can be comfortable until he dies a natural death.

The case described above was one in which the baby went home with his parents, lived for a month, and died peacefully in his mother's arms. This baby was born before the so-called Baby Doe rulings, which cover questions about whether or not severely malformed babies should receive medical treatment. The decisions could be made privately between the parents and the doctor. Through the next several years a number of laws created considerable confusion and heartache for people concerned with babies who were born with deformities. Doctors, hospital workers, parents, and even the federal government became embroiled in determining what should be the right decision, and guidelines were set by those who felt the need to protect the babies. Much of the action centered on infants known as Baby Does.

The first Baby Doe was born on April 9, 1982, in Bloomington Hospital in Bloomington, Indiana. He suffered from Down syndrome, a condition in which there are varying degrees of retardation, and from a condition that made it impossible for food to reach his stomach. He could receive nourishment only intravenously, and the backing up of stomach acid into his lungs would almost certainly cause pneumonia and death within a few days. An operation on his digestive system was needed immediately. The parents were assured that pediatric surgeons were successful in performing the operation to correct digestive problems like his about 90 percent of the time, but the hospital in Bloomington was not equipped for it. There were two medical opinions at this point. The doctor who delivered the baby recommended keeping him in Bloomington Hospital, making him comfortable and free of pain. He and two other obstetricians who agreed with this approach were aware that the baby would die within a short time unless the operation was performed. The pediatric opinion was to transfer the baby to another hospital, where surgery could correct the problem with his digestive system.

The parents of this Baby Doe were told the two conflicting opinions. They refused to give their consent for the operation since they were convinced that a child with Down syndrome had no chance for a meaningful life. Although the pediatricians, who felt this was not true, tried to convince them to allow them to operate, the parents continued to withhold consent. Some legal complications followed. Before they could be resolved, however, the baby starved to death at the age of six days.

The public reacted strongly to the short life and the death of this Baby Doe. Most letters to editors of newspapers nationwide, and most journalists who discussed the case in their columns, protested the action of the parents and the obstetricians. There were cries of infanticide and poignant descriptions of Down-syndrome children whose lives held wonderful meaning, both for themselves and their families. But many people expressed the opinion that the parents of

Baby Doe should be commended for choosing to let their baby die because they loved him enough to let go.

The case of the Bloomington Baby Doe set a far-reaching chain of events into action, including the posting of regulations requiring medical treatment in hospitals and the opening of a hotline for reporting cases of mistreatment of newborns. Most of the reports turned out to be misguided, and there was much concern about the invasion of privacy in dealing with the medical dilemmas of the nursery.

The practice of allowing grossly malformed babies to die existed even long before the Spartans left deformed infants on mountainsides in ancient times. Through the years, many physicians who delivered defective newborns placed them aside, covered them with a towel, and allowed them to die while telling the parents that their babies were badly malformed and stillborn. The doctors made the value judgment about which infants were candidates for treatment and which were candidates for infanticide.

Before the days of modern medical technology, these doctors undoubtedly felt they were saving babies and parents from much suffering, for they knew the babies would soon die, no matter what was done for them. Still, they had to make the decision about which babies could live. With modern medical technology the picture has changed. Many babies with major birth defects can now be saved. Physicians and parents have been forced to make difficult decisions about whether or not to save severely malformed infants. Such was the case with the first Baby Doe and with many babies whose stories have never become public.

Perhaps the most famous Baby Doe was a girl born on October 11, 1983, in St. Charles Hospital in Port Jefferson, New York. This Baby Doe, known as Baby Jane Doe, seemed to symbolize many of the dilemmas involved in neonatal medicine. She was transferred almost immediately to University Hospital at Stony Brook, where there were plans to close the opening that exposed an area of spinal cord in her lower back, a condition known as spina bifida. At some point along the way, the parents learned that their baby also suffered from an abnormally small head and brain, a malformed left foot, paralysis of the legs, and other problems. They refused consent for the surgery to close the opening where her spine was exposed, an operation that would reduce the chances of life-threatening infections, and they also refused permission for the insertion of a shunt to drain fluid from the skull, a procedure for reducing chances of further brain damage. The doctor and the parents agreed to fight infections with antibiotic therapy rather than resort to surgery. This was a time of difficult decisions for the parents, the physicians, and the nurses who worked with Baby Jane Doe, but there was general agreement that the decision not to operate was the most loving and caring one for this severely malformed, brain-damaged baby who could never experience anything in life that is meaningful, but who could experience a great deal of pain.

When Baby Jane Doe was four days old, someone who disagreed with the decision not to operate alerted right-to-life advocate and attorney A. Lawrence Washburn. He and other lawyers became involved in the case, making it known that they felt the need for legal protection of the baby. A long series of legal debates ensued. Although the parents had chosen one course of medical treatment over another, they were harassed at a very difficult time. These concerned and loving parents visited their baby daily as she lay in the newborn intensive care unit of the hospital. While court battles were waged, the parents were comforted somewhat by the fact that they and the hospital were upheld by the courts at almost every stage. Baby Jane Doe went home with her parents after an agreement that a shunt be inserted in her head to drain fluid. But the controversies about this and other Baby Does has continued through the years. The hotline for reporting cases of mistreatment of newborns was dropped, and compromises were made.

In 1984 Congress passed legislation that made withholding "medically indicated" treatment a form of child abuse. Right-to-life groups, associations for the protection of the disabled and handicapped, the American Civil Liberties Union, and numerous other groups have become embroiled in the controversies about imperiled newborns. In some cases, legal guardians have been appointed for malformed newborns, and parents have been deprived of the right to make decisions that would permit them to die. Some people fear that if these severely malformed infants are allowed to die, disabled adults will be threatened. This is an example of a typical "slippery slope" argument.

Exceptions were made in the requirement for medical treatment for three categories of newborns: infants who are irreversibly in a coma, infants for whom medical treatment would just prolong dying, and infants for whom treatment would be futile and its provision inhumane.

Suppose Baby Joe suffers from a severe lack of oxygen during his birth. He will never be able to react to his environment but exists only in an unconscious state. Doctors discover that he has a grave heart defect that could be corrected with surgery, but they agree that the surgery should not be performed since his mental handicap is so severe. Although almost everyone agrees that caregivers should not provide treatment of such a child, there are a comparatively small number of people who feel that as long as a child clings to life, he or she must be treated. Do you feel that the presence of a heartbeat, respiration, or brain activity is reason to make every effort to save a baby's life?

Joseph Fletcher, a Protestant theologian and bioethicist, listed some indicators that he believed apply to humanhood. They include self-awareness, a sense of the future and the past, the capacity to relate to others, concern for others, communication, and curiosity. Do you believe that if a baby will never have the capacity to develop these, the parents should have the right to refuse lifesaving medical treatment? Suppose the doctor has different moral or religious views from those of the parents. Should the doctor be permitted to make the decision about keeping the baby alive? If the doctor decides to keep a severely handicapped baby alive, should he be permitted to do so without the permission of a hospital medical ethics committee which could consider the whole situation objectively?

In June 1986, the United States Supreme Court invalidated the regulations that required federal interventions to make certain that medical treatments were performed on infants born with extreme handicaps. When this ruling was made, Baby Jane Doe, whose spinal gap closed naturally, was still alive, although severely impaired. The 1986 ruling meant that hospitals were not required to post notices encouraging staff members to report denials of treatment to handicapped babies and that federal inspectors known as "Baby Doe squads" could not be involved in the agonizing decisions made by parents and physicians. In most states, child neglect laws require parents to authorize appropriate medical treatment for their children, but the current federal law does not require hospitals to treat handicapped infants without the consent of their parents. This and other laws do not solve or bring an end to the difficult decisions about whether or not to consent to life-prolonging treatment of severely malformed babies. Each case is different, and even medical specialists cannot be certain of the outcome. These are indeed hard choices, and the debate about the care of the critically ill continues.

Helga Kuhse and Peter Singer, authors of *Should the Baby Live?*, believe that the law should interfere in the case of a handicapped infant only if there is a good prospect of that child's living a life free from pain and if the state is prepared to find a home for the child in which enjoyment of such a life is possible, if the parents are not willing or able to provide it. Those who advocate right to life, Kuhse and Singer feel, should be heard only if they are willing to take the responsibility for the quality of life they save. Do you agree?

5

High-Tech Babies

One out of every six couples of childbearing age in the United States has a fertility problem, and most of these people want children. Some want them so desperately that they are willing to undergo considerable emotional turmoil and spend large sums of money even when there is only a small chance that their efforts will be successful. Adoption is not an easy route, especially for those willing to accept only white babies, since there are a hundred or more couples or single would-be adoptive parents for every available white infant. Many who are desperately seeking children turn to new ways of making babies; this is known as the high-tech approach.

The new reproductive technology is a very sensitive area and one of intense controversy. While some procedures are ethical from the medical point of view, certain religious sects disapprove of any procedures that they feel violate the natural method, conception through sexual relations as an expression of love between husband and wife. Many people object only to those methods which involve individuals who are not married to each other, including procedures in which donors remain anonymous, while others feel that any assistance that makes the creation of a life possible is entirely ethical. For them, wanting children is natural, so any procedure used by medical science to make birth possible cannot be unnatural or wrong.

Artificial insemination of a woman by the sperm of an unidentified donor has been traced back to the nineteenth century, but the procedure did not become common until the 1960s. It is now widely accepted in cases where a husband is infertile or carries a serious hereditary disease. In recent years, some single women have preferred artificial insemination as a means of becoming pregnant, and many married couples with medical problems use it.

Although more than 100,000 babies have begun life through artificial insemination, some individuals and groups object strongly to separating babymaking from lovemaking. In many cases, parents hesitate about telling their children that they are not the natural children of the only fathers they have ever known, though they are always the legal children of these fathers.

For many of the 10 million Americans who want babies, artificial insemination is not the answer. There are many instances in which the woman is the infertile partner. Women often succeed in having children through a procedure known as in vitro fertilization.

In vitro fertilization is a relatively new reproductive technology. In the 1970s, British researchers Dr. Patrick Steptoe and Dr. Robert G. Edwards developed a procedure by which eggs could be removed from the ovary of a woman when they were ready for fertilization. After being placed in a glass container, the eggs were fertilized by the husband's sperm and allowed to develop briefly. Then the resulting embryos were inserted into the uterus of the woman from whom the eggs had been removed. Sometimes the mother's body rejected the embryo, but if all went well, one or more embryos would develop normally. About 15 to 20 percent of babies who begin life this way are twins, the result of two viable embryos.

Louise Joy Brown, who became internationally famous as the first "test-tube baby," was born in England on July 25, 1978. Her mother was unable to conceive normally because of damaged fallopian tubes, where fertilization normally takes place. Since the birth of Louise, thousands of babies in the United States, Britain, Australia, and other countries have been born through in vitro fertilization (IVF), and gamete intrafallopian transfer (GIFT). In GIFT, eggs and sperm are placed in a woman's fallopian tube; this allows the sperm to fertilize the egg in natural conditions.

Because the overall success rate for a single in vitro fertilization attempt is very low, the procedure usually needs to be repeated several times before pregnancy occurs. Even then, the success rate is low. To the parents who succeed in having a baby they could not have had without it, the procedure seems like a miracle.

This was true for Matthew's parents. When he was sixteen months old, he and his parents attended a celebration party for families whose babies were born as a result of in vitro fertilization. All of the parents had made many emotional and financial sacrifices to bring their babies into the world, and they were especially proud to have them.

Although in vitro fertilization and intrafallopian transfer are more widely accepted today than they were many years ago, there are still controversies about whether or not it should be practiced at all. Couples who have high-tech babies have often been through a long and expensive ordeal, and they find it rather easy to ignore any unpleasant remarks by those who feel they have been involved in an immoral act because of how their baby was conceived. But some of these parents still fear that a zealot might harm the child who is so precious to them. For example, one set of parents who attended the party for babies who were the result of in vitro fertilization asked the media to identify them only as "the happiest parents in the world."

In addition to religious objections, there were early fears about in vitro fertilization. Some people were afraid of the possibility of undesirable manipulation by medical researchers and experimentation that was not in the best interests of the patients, but that would just provide new information—for instance if a doctor knew that a woman could not carry an embryo to full term but used her in an effort solely to learn something about the medical aspects of the problem without telling her so.

Could a deformed baby be produced by interference with nature? What if clinics were to take advantage of parents who are desperate for a baby? Such fears have been unfounded. In fact, Dr. Steptoe has suggested that stopping research such as his would be comparable to halting the development of airplanes because they made bombing possible.

In their efforts to improve the success rate of in vitro fertilization, doctors learned how to stimulate egg production in women through the use of certain hormones, often called fertility drugs. Four or more eggs are frequently collected during one operation on a woman who has taken the hormones, and all can be fertilized in laboratory glassware. If three embryos are inserted into a woman's uterus and there are one or two viable embryos left in the laboratory, what should doctors do with them? Since these embryos have the potential for becoming human beings, many individuals feel that discarding them is a form of murder. Others point out that every unfertilized egg that is produced in a woman's body has the potential of becoming a human being, and that each cell in the body is a potential embryo and hence a potential human being.

The problem of unneeded embryos has been solved to the satisfaction of some people through the development of a technique that involves freezing the embryos and storing them. If no pregnancy occurs as a result of the first try, even though the embryo was inserted at the time in her monthly cycle when the woman was most likely to become pregnant, the remaining embryos can be thawed and inserted at a similar time in the cycle during another month.

If frozen embryos are not needed because the woman has become pregnant on the first try, and if they are still viable, they might be saved until the woman wants another child, or they might be used for a woman who cannot produce eggs. Before the freezing procedure was developed, all embryos had to be placed in a woman's uterus at once or the unused embryos had to be discarded. If several survived, the problems could be both physical and economic. Discarding these life forms created a moral and ethical dilemma for doctors, while insertion of as many as ten embryos created a problem for the mother, who might have a difficult time with multiple births.

Consider the case of Jane, whose doctor inserted seven embryos into her uterus with the hope that one or two would survive. To everyone's surprise, early in her pregnancy it was learned she was carrying six fetuses. Jane had been trying to become pregnant for three years and there had been many attempts by in vitro fertilization. This was the first time pregnancy had been achieved.

Jane was told that the pregnancy would probably result in miscarriage unless the number of fetuses was reduced. This was very troubling to her. She wanted all the babies, but trying to have them might mean she would have none. Although her doctor did not like the idea of reducing the number of fetuses, he knew that he and his patient must consider the least harm for the most potential good. The choice to abort four of the fetuses was a very difficult one, but Jane and her husband decided in favor of it. Her doctor explained that the fetuses were each about one and a half inches long, and that he would locate them through the use of ultrasound. He would select those that were most accessible and inject potassium chloride into the chest of each by using a needle carefully guided to the proper position. After the injection, each heart would stop and the injected fetuses would die. They would gradually be absorbed into Jane's body, and the two remaining fetuses would have room to grow.

Although there was some risk to Jane and the remaining fetuses in this procedure, everything went well and she gave birth to two healthy babies. At the time, Jane and her husband never told anyone about the procedure, which they felt was very troubling; but when they discussed it with each other, they always felt certain they had made the right choice. Their actions were taken to save the lives of their twins, not to destroy life.

Today, doctors, insurance companies who pay for infertility treatments, and childless couples themselves are pushing for stronger regulations by the medical profession, or by the government, to protect infertile couples from exploitation. The American Fertility Society and the American College of Obstetricians and Gynecologists have established minimum standards for fertility clinics but there is no penalty for not adhering to their guidelines. It costs about $5,000 per couple for each attempt at in vitro fertilization, and success rates for a single attempt at clinics are about 11 for every 100 women. Chances of success vary according to the age of the woman, the nature of her fertility problem, and the skill of the medical staff performing the procedure, but in every case the chance of success is low. Couples who are desperate for a baby are ripe for exploitation, so it is no wonder there is pressure to increase regulations at clinics.

The science of conceiving a baby outside the womb has led to the development of about 200 clinics in the United States with results that vary greatly. In a 1989 report of a survey on fertility clinics, it was shown that some centers had no success rates and others had rates as high as 48 percent. Experts cautioned that some centers specialize in the most difficult cases and there was a need for better standards of evaluation. The survey, undertaken by the Subcommittee on Regulation, Business Opportunities and Energy and the American Fertility Society, was the first to compare procedures at various clinics.

While artificial insemination and in vitro fertilization have gained acceptance, the question of surrogate (substitute) motherhood remains one of considerable controversy. A number of babies have been produced by artificial insemination, using sperm from a father who wanted a child with his genes and the egg of a woman who has agreed to bear the child and surrender it to the natural father. Public awareness of this procedure grew tremendously when Mary Beth Whitehead, now Whitehead-Gould, a surrogate mother, decided that she wanted to break the contract she had signed and keep the baby. The case received wide publicity and the child became famous as Baby M. Court decisions over a period of several years resulted in the awarding of the baby to her natural father and his wife, but visitation rights were given to Mary Beth, who is actually the natural mother but is known as the surrogate mother. Considerable heartbreak was involved for all concerned, and the procedure known as surrogate motherhood was widely discussed. People from all walks of life expressed opinions on this and other cases, and some changed their minds when they considered the problems in depth. Certainly, there are no easy answers.

More than 500 children have been born through surrogate mother arrangements. In some cases, no money was involved. For example, a woman who was artificially inseminated with sperm from her brother-in-law bore a baby for her sister who was unable to have one. In another case, a woman whose daughter was unable to carry a child gave birth to her daughter's babies, a set of triplets. She was implanted with embryos from the eggs of her daughter and sperm of the daughter's husband. In other words, the babies grew in the uterus of their grandmother and were given to her daughter, their mother, at birth.

There can be many variations in a surrogacy arrangement. The woman who carries the baby may have no biological relationship to the child because the egg came from another woman, or she may be the natural mother. She may receive money and become involved partly, or entirely, for this reason. Or she may be motivated by love or compassion for a friend or relative. No matter what the arrangement or the motive, there are people who object to the whole idea of surrogacy.

When women carry babies under a contract to give them up when they are born, the question of selling life arises. On January 27, 1988, Governor James J. Blanchard signed a bill making Michigan the first state to outlaw commercial contracts for women to bear children for others. The National Coalition Against Surrogacy predicts that all commercial contracts for surrogacy will be outlawed within a few years, but many people feel that state laws against it will just drive the procedure underground so that the parties involved will have even less protection.

Ethical issues abound. For many, surrogacy is a totally unacceptable practice. Others feel it should be condoned as long as no money changes hands. They cite the biblical Sarai who sought to satisfy her desire for children through her maidservant, Hagar, and Rachel, who gave her maidservant to Jacob so that she would have a family of her own. In the biblical context, women who volunteered to have a child for another woman were considered blessed. Even so, many people think that surrogate mothering is sinful.

Do you feel that surrogacy is an acceptable procedure if no money changes hands? If laws do not protect all women who are willing to have a baby under contract to someone else, might some be victims of the need for money? Might rich people who are not infertile use surrogacy for the sake of convenience? If surrogacy arrangements are restricted to those people who cannot have children for medical reasons, do you feel it is acceptable? Does surrogacy depersonalize reproduction?

Some advocates of surrogacy feel it is a procedure whose time has come and that it may replace adoption in the future. But in adoption there are fewer unknowns about the health of the baby. What happens to a surrogate baby who is severely handicapped? Will the parents who arranged for it still want the child? Will the mother who delivered it be responsible? Should the child be a responsibility of the state if no one involved in the contract will accept it? Suppose the baby is stillborn? Should the mother still receive the fee? Should surrogacy contracts include a period during which the mother who bore the child could decide to keep the baby? Should the identities of the surrogate and the people seeking her services be kept confidential by an agency so that the parents could never know each other? This might prevent emotional distress if a surrogate tries to claim her child at a later date. These are just some of the problems for which guidelines are needed if surrogacy is to be permitted.

Some people see the brave new world of reproductive technologies as wonderful, while others believe these technologies challenge some deeply held beliefs. There are philosophers, theologians, and medical doctors who feel the time has come to replace the sanctity-of-life ethic (life for life's sake) with a quality-of-life view in which the condition of life is considered. Will this kind of thinking lead to even more serious problems than have already developed? Or will it allow researchers to provide greater help to those whose lives seem incomplete because they cannot have children? How do you feel about research in the areas of cloning and the development of fetuses outside the human body?

The kinds of reproductive techniques that have gained wide acceptance have provided many childless couples with answers to their dreams. They are a far cry from commercial babymaking in which "babies for sale" are produced in large numbers, or attempts at cloning, a procedure in which a new generation would be formed asexually from the cells of one parent. New techniques force society to confront new medical dilemmas, and the ethics of reproduction have become a problem for many facets of society. Should research that can help create families be stopped for fear it may lead to undesirable uses? Or should one remember Dr. Steptoe's remark about not banning the development of airplanes because they can be used as bombers?

6

Experiments on Humans

New procedures save lives, but sometimes they are not the lives of the first patients who give permission for doctors to try the procedures. When is it ethical for a doctor to prescribe a new drug, recommend a new form of surgery, or perform any experimental procedure on a human being?

Innovative operations and other risky procedures on humans are evaluated on the basis of what they can do for the patient and what they can do for future patients. An experiment should be undertaken only when the possible benefits outweigh the risks. Federal rules require that all human subjects give informed consent for their part in medical research, but this was not always the case. Experiments that involved high risk were carried out on many people in nursing homes, hospitals, prisons, and other institutions where the risks were not known to the patients.

One of the most famous scandals of medical research occurred in the 1930s. Certain Public Health Service doctors in Tuskegee, Alabama, left 600 black men with syphilis untreated in order to study the course of their illness. They were observed while they suffered organ damage, degeneration of the nervous system, insanity, and blindness. The men did not know they were part of an experiment. Even though knowing about the experiment might not have led them to seek better treatment, it was unethical for doctors to use them as part of an experiment without their knowledge.

There are many examples of scandalous practices in the past, such as cases in which senile patients were injected with cancer cells or mentally retarded children were deliberately infected with hepatitis. The "experiments" carried out by the Nazis during World War II were called medical, but they were more torture than experiments.

Today hospital review boards or special committees in research institutions weigh the risks and benefits of proposed experiments. When experiments are carried out in the belief that they will help patients, most people are willing to subject themselves, or their loved ones, to some risk.

Many researchers have used themselves in their experiments in attempts to prove their theories. Results have been both helpful and tragic. Sometimes luck plays a part. About a century ago, a distinguished chemist who refused to believe that germs cause cholera swallowed a cupful of virulent cholera germs. He must have had a natural or acquired immunity to cholera, as he did not get sick from the germs which would have caused the disease in most people. His experiment is believed to have played a large part in delaying the acceptance of the bacterial theory of disease. In most cases of self-experimentation, there have been valuable contributions to medical progress. Many examples of researchers who experimented on their own bodies are given in the book *Who Goes First?*

In March 1987, Dr. Daniel Zagury of Pierre and Marie Curie University in Paris reported that he and some volunteers in Africa had been given a vaccine in an experiment in research on AIDS (acquired immune deficiency syndrome).

This disease, which affects the immune system, is caused by a virus. The individuals in the experiment were not infected with it at the time the vaccine, a relatively harmless virus modified to produce a protein found in the AIDS virus, was administered. One year after Dr. Zagury was given the vaccine, laboratory tests were performed on samples of his blood. They showed that the immune factors in the blood samples inhibited two different strains of the AIDS virus from infecting cells. However, there was still no proof that Dr. Zagury's body could have resisted infection by the AIDS virus. In 1988 volunteers in AIDS experiments in the United States produced an immune response to an experimental AIDS vaccine. Although work toward a vaccine against the virus is far from complete, Dr. Zagury and other volunteers are among the people willing to participate in experiments that involve risk.

Most volunteers for medical experiments come from the general public. Many sick individuals are willing to participate in testing new products with the hope they will receive a drug they could not obtain otherwise. After giving their consent to the experiment one group of patients is given the new drug, while another group takes a placebo, non-medicated colored water or a pill resembling the one containing the medication, as a control. Neither patients nor doctors know which group is the control.

Because their immune systems do not function normally, many people with AIDS have taken part in experiments on new drugs for treatment of diseases that attack the body. They hope to help themselves as well as other people with AIDS.

Payment for participation in a medical experiment is another incentive, and such payments are ethical and legal when experiments are conducted by accredited medical institutions. Sometimes advertisements are placed in newspapers asking for volunteers who will receive payment for their part in a special project. Such experiments usually do not carry great risk, but there are volunteers for dangerous experiments too. When a person is dying and there is hope that an experimental procedure will prolong life, or when the quality of life is such that a person would just as soon die as live, the invitation to take a risk is often welcomed as a way to help others who might benefit from the knowledge gained.

Tabatha Fisher had been hospitalized for all three years of her life, and doctors told her parents that she needed the replacement of five abnormal organs to give her a chance at a longer life. Even if a suitable donor could be found, the doctors admitted that such an operation would be a pioneering attempt. Her parents wondered if they should subject her to more suffering when there was so much risk, but they gave permission for the experimental procedure that seemed the only hope for keeping her alive. If you were her parents, would you wonder if the doctors were willing to try this operation only as a challenge to their skills and for the publicity that would follow if the operation succeeded in extending her life? Or would you be willing to take any risk just to keep her alive?

After Tabatha's parents consented, a hospital ethics panel voted by secret ballot to give permission for the procedure. When organs became available from the body of seven-week-old Heather Orick, who died after a car accident, a fifteen-hour operation was performed on Tabatha. After the operation, which took place in the fall of 1987, her vital organs functioned well. She was the third person in the United States to receive so many organs, and the danger of rejection was large. Media coverage was wide; many people hoped and prayed she would survive. In May of 1988, however, Tabatha died after a blood infection caused her heart, liver, lungs, and kidneys to fail in what seemed like a chain reaction.

Since the shortage of suitable organs is so great, some doctors believe that the use of transplant organs from certain animals might save human lives. There is considerable controversy about this subject. In 1984 an attempt was made to save the life of a newborn human by transplanting the heart of a baboon into the tiny body of the infant known only as Baby Fae. She died twenty days after the operation. While many people defended the action as an act of courage that might save the lives of other babies who are born with similar heart defects, there has been much negative criticism. Animal rights groups object to killing baboons, or any kind of animal, for experiments. Doctors pointed out that baboons are not good transplant donors for humans because the animals are not genetically similar. Rejection was one of the problems with Baby Fae. Although it is clear that the immune systems of adults form antibodies against other species, not everyone agrees that this is the case in the immature immune systems of babies. Certainly, Dr. Leonard Lee Bailey, who performed Baby Fae's operation at Loma Linda University Medical Center in California, considered the baboon-to-human heart transplant a reasonable experimental procedure.

Did Baby Fae's parents understand the amount of risk involved in the transplant experiment? Should Dr. Bailey have made a greater effort to find a human heart before transplanting one from a baboon? The experiment on Baby Fae was termed a dramatic one that could pay tremendous dividends, but it was also called a human sacrifice even though she would have died if a human heart had not been found.

The furor created by the Baby Fae case brought about a moratorium on animal-to-human transplants. Still, a number of researchers have continued to experiment with cross-species transplants in a variety of animals. Since donor infant hearts are scarce, Dr. Bailey foresees the use of baboon hearts as bridges to human heart transplants for thousands of babies who need new hearts in order to live.

Three years after Dr. Bailey created a furor by transplanting the baboon heart into Baby Fae, he made headlines as the world's leading surgeon for infant heart transplants. Of the eleven babies who were given new hearts through Dr. Bailey's surgical skill, eight were alive two years later. He and other doctors would like to do more heart transplants on infants if organs were available. Infant donors are scarce in part because it is hard to determine brain death in babies.

Suppose you were a medical doctor treating Mr. Z, who is suffering from Parkinson's disease. His muscles are so rigid that he cannot brush his teeth, write, feed himself, or carry on other everyday activities. He cannot walk from his bed to the bathroom, nor can he speak clearly. You have tried every drug that is normally used in the treatment of Parkinson's disease, but some do no good and others make him sick. The part of his brain that produces dopamine, a chemical that carries messages between neurons, is not producing enough of it. An inadequate amount reaches the part of his brain that controls muscle action and other functions. Why not just inject dopamine, or just give pills of it? There is a blood-brain barrier that protects the brain, and the dopamine will pass through it. A related drug, L-dopa, does reach the brain and has been proven effective for a limited period of time, but Mr. Z cannot tolerate larger doses.

Mr. Z has heard that surgeons at a distant hospital are experimenting with Parkinson's patients using transplants to

replace dying tissue in their brains. You know that this procedure is very experimental and results may not be lasting.
Would you feel that Mr. Z is able to give informed consent if
he is accepted for such an operation?

In spite of the experimental nature of brain implants,
thousands of requests for this kind of treatment reach the
American Parkinson Disease Association each year. These
patients do not care if the operation is new and there is no
track record about how long improvement will last. They are
willing to take the risk, with the hope that the treatment will
help them.

Perhaps the most dramatic experiment on humans was the
introduction of an artificial heart into a human being. This
followed a number of human heart transplants, but if an artificial heart could be perfected, problems such as organ
shortage and tissue rejection might be partly eliminated. On
December 1, 1982, after years of planning and research,
Barney Clark became the first human to receive an artificial
heart. Much of the world watched for news of the outcome
of this dramatic operation, which was performed at the University of Utah Medical Center, with a plastic-and-Velcro
device known as the Jarvik-7, named after Dr. Robert Jarvik,
its inventor. Dr. Clark, a sixty-one-year-old retired dentist
who was dying from heart disease, seemed an ideal candidate for the experiment. He was willing to have his own
heart replaced with a mechanical heart with full knowledge
that he would be tethered to a bulky, noisy machine for the
rest of his life. At the time of the operation, and for the fif-
teen weeks that followed, most people hailed the experiment
as a major step in the advancement of medicine. When complications arose there was less enthusiasm, but Barney Clark
lived with his artificial heart for a total of 112 days.

While Barney Clark's artificial heart was beating, as it did about 12 million times, there was little negative criticism about the experiment. After Dr. Clark died, and other recipients of artificial hearts suffered strokes and other complications that led to death within a short time, questions arose about the ethics of the artificial-heart program.

Those experts who support the program point out that there are from 15,000 to 30,000 people who would be better off with new hearts but there are donors for only about 1 percent of them. Mass-produced artificial hearts could eliminate the problem of a shortage of organs, but the time for such mass production, if it ever comes, is far in the future.

People in favor of the program point out that Barney Clark and other recipients of artificial hearts are being rescued "from the brink of death." Critics say that no doctor can actually predict the exact longevity of an ailing heart. There is controversy about whether or not patients might live longer without a mechanical heart than with one. In any case, the quality of life after an implant is still considered so poor that any gain for patients is in question. Consider what life must be like for someone tethered to a machine, with a constant thudding in the chest. The hope of helping to develop a better artificial heart provides some motivation for recipients.

What about experiments in which artificial hearts are used as bridges until compatible human hearts are available for transplant? Although this kind of human experiment is generally praised, there are critics here too. Professor George J. Annas of Boston University Schools of Medicine and Public Health suggests the following scenario: A thousand people are waiting for human heart transplants and only 600 hearts are available for transplant this year. The people who do not get transplants get mechanical hearts to tide them over. They top the waiting list, so the next year the first 400 hearts go to them. But another thousand people need hearts in the new year, and only 600 are available. Using 400 to replace the artificial hearts leaves just 200 for them. So now 800 people need mechanical hearts. And so on. In other words, as long as there is a shortage of human hearts available for transplant, the use of mechanical hearts as a bridge affects only who will get the hearts, not how many will benefit from them. Of course, for the people who need them, the picture does not look the same. About a third of the patients who wait in vain for heart transplants die within three months, and almost all of them die within a year. Researchers hope that using artificial hearts as bridges could extend their lives. By early 1989, artificial hearts and heart-assist devices had been planted as bridges in 200 patients worldwide.

Dr. Christiaan Barnard, the South African surgeon who performed the first human heart transplant in 1976 and who is now scientist-in-residence at the Oklahoma Transplant Institute, suggests that someday animal hearts may take the place of artificial hearts until a human heart is available for transplant. If the problem of rejection can be conquered, someday it may be feasible to use the hearts of pigs, goats, and calves that are scheduled for slaughter. But by then, totally implantable electric-powered artificial hearts may be perfected.

Cost is another factor in dispute in the evaluation of artificial-heart programs. Soon after it was decided to end the artificial-heart program, largely because of its tremendous cost and the limited number of people it would serve, pressure from some members of Congress forced reinstatement of the program for a short time, but permanent implants of artificial hearts have been halted because of bad results. New techniques are extremely expensive, and the long-term benefits are uncertain. Many experts feel that money would be better spent on the prevention of heart disease and other illnesses, but efforts in preventing health problems bring less dramatic results.

In the face of death, many men and women are willing to act as guinea pigs for techniques that may bring better lives to others in years to come. However, ethics committees and public watchdogs are considering heart transplant procedures as well as others more cautiously than they have in the past. They are less likely to give permission for the fast experimental track.

What about patients who are unable to make informed decisions because of special problems? Today's guidelines protect from human experimentation children, the mentally ill, the retarded, and others who cannot give informed consent, but the line between treatment and experimentation can be thin.

Suppose you are asked to join a committee that is working toward better laws in the area of informed consent. Does a parent have a right to decide that a child undergo experimental surgery? How can parents know if permission for the operation is based on saving the child or serving science? Who will guide them objectively? A journalist has indicated that one might conclude Baby Fae's body was donated alive to science. Adults who are "going to die anyway" may be willing to take part in an experiment that offers a slight chance of keeping them alive. This can be informed consent. But what about the children and other people who are not competent to decide for themselves? Would you support a group that works to protect children from medical experiments? Or do you feel that a child should have that slight chance too?

7

Some Transplant Controversies

How would you feel if you saw the following ad in your local newspaper?

> WANTED: Kidney from healthy donor. Will pay $15,000 for kidney with proper match. Call between 10 A.M. and 4 P.M. Monday through Friday.

Although buying a kidney, or any other organ, is illegal in the United States, there are countries in which selling organs has become a way out of poverty. Interviews in twenty-three countries have revealed that the average price for a kidney is $13,000, far more that the cost of an equal weight (about five ounces) of gold. Healthy kidneys separate wastes from the other materials in the blood, making elimination through the urinary tract possible. If the wastes are not removed, a person dies. Someone who needs a kidney may be willing to pay, and a person who needs money may be willing to sell one and hope that the remaining kidney will function as long as it is needed.

Occasionally, people who want to sell one of their own organs ask for sums ranging from $5,000 to $100,000 and more. One man proposed a commercial venture for the buying and selling of kidneys in the United States, a business he claimed would provide a service that could save many lives.

The American Kidney Foundation and other ethical organizations involved with transplants hold that it is immoral and unethical to place a living person at the risk of surgery in return for a cash payment. The buying and selling of organs is very different from what doctors had in mind when they performed the first successful kidney transplant in 1954.

When Richard Herrick was dying of kidney failure, doctors had transplanted about twenty kidneys without success. The new kidneys were rejected by the immune systems of the patients who received them, even when the donor was a sibling. Richard Herrick had an identical twin, Ronald, who expressed a desire to give him one of his kidneys. After a skin graft from Ronald to Richard was successful, it was believed there was a good chance that a kidney from Ronald would not be rejected by Richard. Doctors operated on them just two days before Christmas.

In one operating room a surgeon removed Ronald's left kidney, while a surgeon in the next room prepared Richard's body to receive it. In about an hour, the healthy kidney was attached to veins and arteries, which allowed blood to circulate through it, and a connection was made to Richard's bladder. Clear urine began to flow. This had happened in operations on other individuals, but their bodies gradually rejected the new kidney tissue. Not so with Richard. He lived eight years after the transplant and died from heart disease.

By the time Richard died in 1962, scientists had discovered drugs that suppress tissue rejection, and compatibility became less of an issue. Today thousands of kidney transplants are performed each year in the United States alone. In one recent year, out of almost 9,000 kidneys only four were transferred from one identical twin to the other.

The success of transplants today is due partly to a drug, cyclosporine, that was introduced in 1980 as an immune-system suppressant. Although it prevents the organ recipient from rejecting a new organ, patients must take the drug for the rest of their lives, and this increases their risk of infection. Cyclosporine has also been linked to kidney damage. Doctors now use smaller doses of cyclosporine than in earlier years and combine it with other antirejection drugs. New techniques allow doctors to take a tiny piece of tissue and check it for signs of rejection after transplants.

Cyclosporine is not a part of the organ transplant controversy. Thousands of people are now living with someone else's heart beating in their chests. Transplant surgery is considered one of the greatest advances in modern medicine. Although there is a high success rate for transplants, the problem of obtaining organs remains. Today some 12,000 people are on waiting lists for kidneys and must rely on dialysis machines to remove wastes from their bodies. Since many hospitals are not equipped with dialysis machines, patients must often travel a long distance three times a week for a four-hour session in which they are hooked to a machine.

The scarcity of organs has raised some hard questions about who should receive transplants. Take the case of a baby who is dying because her heart is defective. Her doctor tells the parents that a transplant might save the child, and they immediately give consent for such an operation. The doctor approaches the hospital panel, but after careful consideration, panel members reject the patient as a good candidate for a transplant and admit the rejection is due partly to the shortage of organs. The doctor is disappointed and the baby's parents are desperate.

The parents manage to persuade a television producer to

let them make their plea for a heart for their baby on a local television program. This kind of drama attracts a large number of viewers, and in this case a spokesman from another hospital calls in the middle of the show to say that the hospital has a heart that could be used by this baby. The studio viewing audience cries tears of joy.

Few people who are watching the program think of the thousands who are waiting for organs that they will never receive. Media publicity finds organs for a few, and sometimes appeals to famous people accomplish the same thing. Not everyone can find an organ this way. Should some people be allowed to appeal publicly while others who may have been waiting longer are unable to reach the public ear? Not everyone agrees.

Suppose the baby described earlier was rejected by the hospital panel because the parents were drug addicts. One of the qualifications that ethics committees consider is the home situation. Will the patient have good care after the operation? If the parents are both drug addicts, they may not be able to handle the difficult days and months ahead because they spend much of their time obtaining the illegal drugs they crave. The heart given to their baby may have deprived another child, whose chances of life after the operation might have been much better. So media publicity may ignore one of the criteria for selection and actually promote the use of transplant surgery in cases where it is of little lasting benefit. The person who receives the transplant may not be able to take advantage of it because of personal or financial problems. Many medical experts feel strongly that all organ procurement should be conducted through scientific, medical channels. The United Network for Organ Sharing is a nonprofit agency in Richmond, Virginia, that was authorized by Congress in 1984 to oversee and improve the distribution and procurement system. Its computers list the name, blood type, and other information for each of the many thousands of people who are waiting for organs.

Media publicity does increase awareness of the need for more organs to be used for transplant. About 100,000 people are on dialysis for kidney failure. Not all of them are candidates for transplants, but many more organs are needed. Although more than a thousand heart transplants are done in a year, there are estimates that 12,000 to 14,000 could be done if organs were available. About 25,000 of the people who die in the United States each year could serve as donors of various organs, but organs are harvested from only about 2,500 of them.

Success rates for transplant operations continue to rise, and in some cases, several lives are saved with organs from a single person. Lungs might go to one person, the liver to another, the heart to another, and kidneys to two others. Single individuals may receive a number of new organs at one time too.

As success with transplants increases, so do waiting lists. Many patients die in hospitals while they are waiting for organs to become available for them. Some outpatients, who know that they will die soon if the organs they need do not become available, wear buzzers that alert them to the arrival of a suitable donor organ at their hospital. Sometimes the beeper goes off accidentally, creating terrible disappointments, but when an organ really does come, teams at the hospital act fast. The recipient is rushed to the hospital where the transplant will take place, while organs are chilled and flown from the donor's hospital in a cooler. They are brought to the transplant patient's operating room, where surgeons may have already begun the preparation by removing the defective organ. Time is an important factor, for a kidney should be transplanted within twenty-four to seventy-two hours and a donor liver has a life of only eight to twelve hours after removal. For some organs the time is even shorter.

Polls indicate that from 45 to 70 percent of people are willing to donate their organs at death, but relatively few have signed donor cards that make their willingness known. Many states have a form on the back of driver's licenses, and forms are available from the American Medical Association, the Red Cross, and hospitals. Families should be informed of a person's wishes too. Suppose Jed was killed in an automobile accident. He had expressed his wishes to have his organs used to help others if such a thing should happen, but he had not told his family. His organs could not be used because his family was unaware of his wishes and would not give consent.

According to a law that went into effect in October 1987, all hospitals in the United States that receive federal Medicare or Medicaid benefits must identify patients who could donate organs and tissues and solicit organ donations. By 1988 at least forty states had passed laws requiring the hospitals to solicit organs from families of potential candidates. All hospitals that transplant organs had to become members of a national organ-sharing network. But many hospitals have lagged in putting the new laws into effect.

Health workers continue to shy away from broaching the subject of organ donation with families at their time of grief. New training programs are recommended to help physicians, nurses, clergy, and social workers overcome their nervousness. According to one study, 70 percent of families who are asked about donating a relative's organs give permission. A few months after the California legislature passed a law requiring health workers to make the request, there was a 50-

percent increase in organ donations. However, much more remains to be done.

Many families find comfort in knowing that the organs of a loved one mean life for another person. Brenda Winner was a compassionate person who hoped to help others. When she was five months pregnant, she learned that the baby she was carrying was missing most of its brain, a condition known as anencephaly. Although she knew her baby would live only a short time after birth, she chose to carry the baby to full term with the hope that some other baby would be able to live because of organs donated from her child. Her baby was stillborn and only the heart valves and corneas could be used, but the case sparked new awareness of the controversy about infant organ donors.

Several thousand anencephalic babies are born each year, and many parents of these babies are eager to derive some meaning from their own heartbreaking experiences by having organs of their own babies used in transplants so that other babies can live. There is a shortage of organs for the very young, and it is estimated that 40 to 70 percent of children on transplant waiting lists die before organs can be found for them.

In most cases, the organs of anencephalic babies have deteriorated so much by the time death occurs that they cannot be used for transplants. Doctors experiment with techniques to maintain their organs with life support systems while the babies are still alive. However, some ethicists object to keeping a baby alive on a support system just so the organs can be harvested. By law, all organ donors must be brain dead, and anencephalics who are not stillborn do not always meet this criterion at the very beginning of their lives. The stalk of nerve fibers that functions regulates their sleeping and waking, and lets them cry and suck; but as their brain stems stop functioning, they breathe sporadically and their organs become oxygen-starved. Thus they deteriorate and cannot be used for transplants.

Do you feel that brain-death laws should be amended to declare anencephalic babies dead so that their organs can be used? Should those parents who wish to have their anencephalic babies' organs used to save lives have the choice of doing so?

While corneas for grafting into damaged eyes can be donated by almost anyone, other organs must come from donors who meet certain criteria. A donor must be under the age of fifty-five and must have been healthy before having suffered permanent cessation of all brain functions. Usually, donors are people who have suffered head injuries from a car or motorcycle accident, a gunshot wound, or a blood vessel bursting in the brain.

Suppose you were asked to give permission for the use of the organs of a loved one to save the lives of others. How would you decide? Might you worry about the possibility of a team of surgeons harvesting organs before the person was really dead? Although he has been pronounced dead, his heart may continue to beat with oxygen supplied by a mechanical respirator. You are told that his organs can be kept functioning for a matter of days with the aid of a machine. Is the loved one really dead if he hasn't taken his last breath? (A chest goes up and down when a patient has mechanical support, even though there is brain death.)

You may have other reservations too. You might ask if the donation will mean that a viewing will be possible. You will be assured that it is, and that any kind of funeral service is still possible, including one with an open casket.

Does the idea of opening the body to harvest the organs upset you? New attitudes are changing the image of organ donation from something macabre to an act of compassion and love. Many people are willing to give permission for the donation of organs when they feel the donor would want this done if he or she could make the choice.

In spite of a trend toward acceptance, not everyone agrees it is morally right to transplant organs. Some people believe a person's body is a gift from God and interpret this to mean that no one may choose to be mutilated by giving up an organ unless it is for the welfare of his or her own body. Certainly, a donation cannot help the dead person. On the other hand, there are people who believe it is not morally right to refuse the gift of life to those who are waiting for organs. As many as five lives may be saved by the donation of organs from one person who has died. Kidney patients can rely on machines until kidneys deteriorate, but those needing hearts, livers, and pancreases will most likely die soon if no organ is found for them.

Doctors will not take the organs from a person, even though that person has signed a donor card, if the family feels uncomfortable about their doing so. Sometimes a family wants a say in who receives the organs donated by a loved one, but the hospital staff may not approve. The family's intended recipient may not even be suitable medically. Does a family really own the organs of a relative who has died? In some European countries, there is a system of presumed consent, which allows the state to harvest organs from anyone who dies in a hospital.

Sometimes people do not realize that organs cannot be used for recipients indiscriminately. Missie, the daughter of an accident victim who is not expected to live, will agree to the use of her father's liver only for a boy she has read about in the local paper. She does not realize that his liver must be the right size or it cannot be connected to the proper blood vessels. Although there are cases in which a person who is dying specifies the use of an organ for a particular individual, this is not always practical. In addition to size and blood type, there is the matter of time. New preservation methods for transplant organs are now being tested. With experimental techniques, donated livers and pancreases have been kept alive for twenty-seven hours before being transplanted. This is roughly nineteen hours longer than current methods, allowing more time for checking donor organs for AIDS, hepatitis, and other infectious diseases, and for the recipient and the organ to reach each other.

Many factors determine how organs are used. But there are still difficult questions when there is more than one organ match for several needy recipients. In some cases, social values and ability to pay play a part in deciding who receives an organ. Doctors might consider the family situation, the patient's future in terms of contribution to society, his or her character, and ability to pay. A heart transplant may cost over $100,000 and a liver transplant over $200,000. Even if financial aid is available for the operation, what about care afterward? Should people be denied available organs because they cannot pay?

Today doctors do not have to "play God" in determining who gets an organ, because they can follow guidelines. A formula for assigning organs other than kidneys includes points for medical urgency, for the logistics of bringing the patient and the organ together, for blood-type compatibility, and for time on the waiting list. Usually the organ goes to the patient who scores the highest.

In some hospitals heart patients are placed on a list according to blood type and through an evaluation system that ranks them from 1 to 6, those in the 6 category being on a heart pump or other mechanical life support. As their conditions worsen, the patients move up the list, but as many as a third die before they reach the point that they are eligible for a donor heart and one is ready for them.

Still, there are questions about how to make the best use of an organ. Should it go to the person who needs it most because he or she is near death or to the person who can get the most use from it? Is it fair to give an organ to a person who is known for disobeying doctor's orders and who says he will not take medication to forestall organ rejection?

8

AIDS: Some New
Dilemmas

AIDS (acquired immune deficiency syndrome) is a subject of controversy on many fronts. In addition to being a medical issue, it is a public health crisis, an issue in the workplace, an economic concern, a social problem, and a human tragedy. The AIDS virus has infected an estimated 1.5 million people in the United States, over 100,000 of them had developed the full-blown disease by July 1989, and more than half of these had died. No one knows how many people who carry the virus may eventually develop symptoms, but the percentage is expected to be very large, perhaps 100 percent.

AIDS is spread through sexual activity, by transfer of blood, and from pregnant mothers to their babies, but no one has ever proved it is spread by casual contact.

Even in the early years after the recognition of AIDS in 1981, attitudes about it varied from compassion for the ill to feelings that God was punishing those who had sinned. Most of the people who suffer from AIDS contracted the disease through sharing unclean needles in intravenous drug use, or through homosexual activity not accepted by some people. A smaller percentage of people with AIDS contracted it through blood transfusions before blood was screened for the virus or through heterosexual relations with people who had the virus. Many children with AIDS were infected by their mothers before or during birth; others were infected through blood transfusions.

In spite of widespread attempts to educate people about the way AIDS is spread, many have refused to believe that it could not be spread by casual contact. Even in 1988, a hospital policy of allowing doctors and nurses with AIDS to care for patients provoked much controversy. A 1989 survey showed that many children mistakenly believed that AIDS was spread by insects, toilets, drinking fountains, and giving blood.

"Why should I believe the experts when they do not even know all the facts about AIDS?" many people ask, for no cure has been found and the disease is still spreading. Actually, the experts have an amazing amount of information about AIDS. They know that the damaged immune systems of people with AIDS cannot do normal battle with infections; they know how the disease is spread and not spread; they know much about AIDS viruses; they are developing more drugs that help the sick; and they are working toward a vaccine that may prevent AIDS. There are tests to show the presence of antibodies that form when a person has been exposed to the AIDS virus. Guidelines have been set for the public, for health workers, for the courtroom, and for schools.

Although most people who have developed antibodies from exposure have no symptoms, they can spread the disease. Most people with AIDS are reliable, but what about people who refuse to obey the guidelines? Such cases are relatively unusual, but they can create serious and complex problems.

Kathy, a woman who had frequent sexual involvement

with members of the armed forces, was told by a health care worker that she was carrying the AIDS virus and that she could spread it through unprotected sexual behavior. Kathy did not feel sick, and she wanted to continue to enjoy her brand of social life. She knew she might develop full-blown AIDS and die from diseases that would invade her body because her immune system was weakened. But Kathy was afraid her male companions would leave if she warned them she carried the virus and could spread it. She was not willing to harm her relationship with them.

Legal cases have been filed accusing people of trying to transmit the virus by sexual acts, biting, or spitting, but they are relatively rare. Some laws have been passed, and many more have been considered, for making it criminal to knowingly expose people to the AIDS virus. Colorado and Indiana have passed laws that permit people with AIDS to be isolated if they refuse to desist from "dangerous conduct."

Many public health officials and other experts believe that the movement to criminalize the transmission of AIDS is based on political eagerness to do something to prevent the spread of the disease. Fortunately, most people who test positive for antibodies that indicate they have been exposed to the virus take precautions so they will not spread the disease.

But AIDS presents other dilemmas. One of these concerns is educating people to avoid the spread of AIDS and persuading them to change their behavior. In May of 1988, the federal government began a three-week campaign to inform Americans about AIDS. In addition to messages on television and posters in every post office, a pamphlet about what everyone needs to know about AIDS was mailed to the 107 million households served by the United States Postal Service. Efforts were made to distribute a Spanish edition in

Latin neighborhoods and to get the pamphlet to people with no fixed mailing addresses, such as the homeless. Many schools across the country have included educational programs in their curricula, with some schools beginning in kindergarten. News media continue to include educational programs and short public affairs messages on the subject. While education is showing positive results in the homosexual population and the incidence of cases among gay men appears to be slowing in some cities, much remains to be done to prevent the spread of a disease that will be with us for many years to come.

While many homosexuals are acting responsibly, changing the behavior of intravenous drug users has proved especially difficult, and in New York City, for one, the AIDS virus has spread more rapidly among intravenous drug users than any other group. Addicts spread the disease through the use of dirty needles and through sexual relations. Bisexuals and women with AIDS can pass the disease to their sexual partners, and women have a 30- to 50-percent chance of infecting the babies they bear. In a 1988 study in New York City, 1 in 61 babies was found to have been exposed to the AIDS virus. Most of these children were born to drug users. In another study, published in 1989, as many as 1 in 25 mothers in the South Bronx, New York City, had the AIDS virus, showing AIDS had spread widely in impoverished neighborhoods where there was rampant drug use.

The issue of giving clean needles to addicts in an effort to help prevent the spread of AIDS has been one of considerable controversy. In Europe free needles have been supplied to addicts for this reason, but many health workers in the United States have resisted the practice, thinking it would promote drug abuse. There is fear that addicts would sell the sterile needles and continue to share used needles in a traditional way in so-called shooting galleries. Others feel the distribution of free needles would be a means of protecting the public and saving lives. When a pilot program for the distribution of free needles to addicts in New York City was approved in 1988, it was estimated that as many as 60 percent of the city's 200,000 addicts carried the AIDS virus. By supplying sterile needles or kits of bleach to clean needles, health experts hope to get the addicts into treatment. When more treatment programs are available, more addicts can be tested and counseled on a regular basis. Drug addiction has been called the gateway for AIDS to the heterosexual population, but there is disagreement about the way to stop the spread of the disease among addicts and their sexual contacts.

Testing is a matter of heated debate too. Some groups in the United States are already subject to routine testing for AIDS antibodies. For example, members of the armed forces might need to give blood in an emergency and there would be no time to screen their blood for antibodies to the virus. Recruits are tested to prevent complications from the protective vaccines they receive when they enlist. People with AIDS are rejected. Since immigrants with any contagious disease are denied entry to the United States, it is not surprising to find routine testing of immigrants for AIDS.

Many people have advocated mandatory testing of people who apply for marriage licenses, but others point out that young heterosexual couples are not considered high risk. There is a very low prevalence of infection in the general population. In those states that passed laws requiring testing of marriage license applicants, this expensive procedure identified very few people with AIDS.

People who feel that money for AIDS prevention could be spent more wisely in other ways point out that many states have repealed the requirement for premarital blood tests for syphilis because so few cases of this venereal disease were detected this way.

Many experts are in favor of testing for groups who practice high-risk behavior. Homosexual organizations have provided considerable education and there has been evidence of changed behavior among homosexuals. It has been shown that even though many homosexuals have encounters with numerous partners, there are others who have been in a faithful relationship with one lover for many years. They are at less risk than heterosexuals with many different partners. However, drug abusers have been less cooperative about behavior changes, and there is concern about their spreading the disease among the heterosexual population. Most babies with AIDS have mothers who are drug abusers or who are sexual partners of drug abusers. Testing of addicts is difficult unless they are in treatment, and control of AIDS is one of the reasons many people are urging an increase in the number of drug treatment centers.

In the past, testing was not widely endorsed by physicians and advocates for homosexual rights because it was believed that knowing one was infected would not help medically and it would risk breaches of confidentiality that might result in the loss of homes, jobs, friendships, and insurance coverage. However, in April of 1989, experts announced that improved treatments for AIDS were a powerful reason for those at high risk to be tested, even if they had no symptoms. In some cases, early treatment might stave off infections and ease the amount of suffering that comes with full-blown AIDS.

Testing of hospital patients is encouraged, especially by doctors who want a complete picture of their patients' health and by those who are concerned about exposure to themselves and other health care providers. Surgeons who are exposed to large amounts of patients' blood are at risk even though they wear gloves, for the gloves are often punctured by sharp instruments and bone fragments. Dentists too may be at risk. By 1988, so many health workers were wearing surgical gloves for protection against the AIDS virus that a temporary glove shortage developed.

A controversy exists about whether or not doctors are obliged to care for patients with AIDS. While it has been pointed out that physicians have died along with their patients in other epidemics and in warfare, many voices have been raised about the obligations of physicians to perform elective operations on patients who carry the AIDS virus when large amounts of blood are involved. Do such procedures pose an unacceptable risk to members of a medical staff whose services are needed to save the lives of large numbers of people? Routine testing of hospital patients who are candidates for surgery has been proposed as a safeguard, but not everyone agrees that this is ethical. The Texas Medical Association has adopted a policy in which doctors who do not feel an obligation to treat people with AIDS may refer them to someone who is willing to do so. Whether or not a doctor is required to treat a patient is considered a new ethical question, one that was not raised before the appearance of AIDS.

While there are questions about the rights of health care workers, there are also questions about the rights of patients. A positive test for AIDS in a patient's medical history may make it impossible for the person to obtain health or life insurance. The right of insurance companies to know about a person's exposure to the AIDS virus is in itself controversial. Insurance companies point out that some of them have insisted on physicals and have refused to accept individuals with life-threatening diseases such as cancer, diabetes, and heart disease. They claim that a person who tests positive for the AIDS virus is twenty-six times more likely to die within seven years than is the average American. Those opposed to testing feel that insurers cannot guarantee confidentiality and that a breach of it to someone who tests positive can be devastating.

What about anonymous testing of hospital patients to help determine the extent of the disease? This kind of testing is being done in a number of studies in an effort to forecast the future and provide better medical services for those who will need them. In December 1987, federal health officials announced a plan to collect blood samples in thirty major cities from selected hospitals and clinics for sexually transmitted diseases, drug addiction, family planning, pregnancy, and tuberculosis. Blood from 1.6 million people will be tested annually, but there will be no identification other than age, sex, race, and area of residence. Some universities have agreed to anonymous testing for the purpose of determining the degree to which AIDS has spread.

Because anonymity protects the privacy of participants, there is no way of informing those whose tests are positive, but this project and others will help to estimate the extent of the epidemic. In the case of newborns at any hospital, blood that is obtained from heel pricks for a number of routine diagnostic tests on babies can be used to test for AIDS.

Although random testing of blood from anonymous donors is valuable for some purposes, most public health officials agree that people with positive tests for the AIDS antibody should be informed, counseled, and educated about the behavior necessary to avoid spreading the virus. In some places, people who test positive are urged to identify their sexual partners so that they can be warned of their risk of infection and the need to be tested. If people are embarrassed to identify those who might have been exposed, health officials will volunteer to notify them with the message that "someone who loves you has tested positively for the AIDS antibody." A new policy of the American Medical Association holds that doctors have a responsibility to ensure that sexual partners of those who test positive are informed. This has been called a landmark move in medical ethics, but the severity of the public health problem was thought to outweigh confidentiality.

Voluntary rather than mandatory testing appeals to most health workers because they fear many who are at high risk would go underground to avoid testing and would not seek treatment or change their behavior to avoid the spread of AIDS. If the disease is driven underground, it will be harder to control. An important aspect of today's public health program is the cooperation of vulnerable persons and protection of their records. Without confidentiality, people who carry the virus may lose their jobs and their homes, and may face social ostracism.

Quarantine for those who carry the virus has been suggested as a way to control the spread of the AIDS epidemic, and in some states, bills have been introduced to try to put this draconian plan into action. In Cuba, people carrying the AIDS virus have been isolated on a farm outside Havana. However, most health experts insist that AIDS does not fit the pattern of diseases for which quarantine makes sense. The 1.5 million people in the United States who are believed to carry the virus may or may not develop AIDS. Within five years, there may be between 50 and 100 million people worldwide who are infected with the virus, according to projections by the World Health Organization. With this kind of outlook, arguments for isolation seem ridiculous. Perhaps those who want to quarantine people who carry AIDS do so partly from fear and partly from a desire to punish. Usually it is fear that provokes the quarantine argument for children with AIDS.

Generally, quarantine is considered practical only as a last resort for the relatively few individuals who persist in endangering others even after counseling. Civil liberties groups and public health officials say that quarantine will have little effect on the spread of AIDS. Quarantine and testing continue to be subjects of debate.

In the United States, citizens are protected by the Fourth Amendment, which holds that the government should not be able to interfere with a person's liberty or invade his or her privacy without "probable cause" that makes the government believe the person has committed a crime. But protection of public health is still considered of primary importance, and some courts may view serious burdens on civil rights as part of the price of living in today's society. AIDS poses a special challenge for health policy makers who must find ways of ensuring public safety while protecting individual rights.

The epidemic of fear that has been called more dangerous than the AIDS epidemic itself may continue to decrease as education increases. This seems to be true in dealing with children of school age, but the controversy about allowing children with AIDS to attend school has been long and bitter. In some states, children with AIDS have been protected by law from discrimination, but policies and attitudes vary greatly. One of the most famous cases of discrimination against children with AIDS is that of the Ray family, whose three sons were believed to have been infected with the AIDS virus from treatment for their hemophilia with blood products before such products were screened. After the three boys were refused admission to public school in Arcadia,

Florida, the Rays' house was burned. When they first stayed in a hotel after the incident, the maids refused to clean their rooms. But in Sarasota, where the public school district had approved a measure allowing children with AIDS to attend school, they were welcomed.

As studies continue to show that AIDS has never been spread by casual contact, and as laws force parents and school staffs around the country to accept children with AIDS, the hysteria has lessened somewhat.

AIDS has brought many new medical and ethical dilemmas since it was first discovered. Extensive studies guide policymakers in their efforts to protect public health and the rights of individuals. But efforts to increase education about AIDS will be needed for many years to come, for the peak years of the epidemic are still in the future.

9

The Right to Die

Until Mrs. F. was ninety-three years old, she was alert and active, she cared for herself, and her mind was still sharp and clear. She became more frail over the next few years and had to be hospitalized several times with pneumonia and heart problems. Every time she got sick, she complained that she was too old, tired of living, and said that she wanted to die in her sleep. She hated being ill and dependent on others. But she always received excellent care in the hospital, and the doctors always cured the pneumonia.

At age ninety-six, she had a stroke and was sent to a nursing home because she could no longer care for herself; she needed to be fed, bathed, and clothed. She recognized her family when they visited, but was too confused to engage in conversation. She did not know where she was living. Unable to read or knit, she watched television without comprehending. Her life had become a meaningless, vegetative existence.

If Mrs. F. had fallen ill with pneumonia at the end of the last century, the scenario might have been very different. She probably would have died at home, surrounded by loving relatives who would have considered her death a sad but natural ending after a long and vigorous life. Even as recently as the middle of the twentieth century, about half the deaths in the United States occurred at home. By the end of the 1980s, four out of every five people died in hospitals, nursing homes, or other institutions.

In earlier times, doctors did not have antibiotics or complicated machinery to keep people alive, and elderly people often died of pneumonia; in fact, pneumonia was frequently called the "old man's friend." The definition of death was simple. When a person stopped breathing or his heart stopped, he was dead. As late as 1968, *Black's Law Dictionary* defined death as a "total stoppage of the circulation of the blood, and a cessation of the animal and vital functions consequent thereon." By the early 1950s, however, the invention of the heart-lung machine had made it possible for doctors to stop a patient's heart and perform open-heart surgery while the machine did the job of keeping the blood circulating. Some people concluded that such a patient must therefore have "died" and then was brought back to life when the surgeon restarted the heart after finishing the operation. With these machines, doctors could also keep people alive indefinitely, even if they had suffered irreversible brain damage.

But is a person really alive if his or her brain is dead? Some experts have pointed out a distinction between the whole biological organism and the "person," that is, the part that makes an individual a human being with thoughts, feelings, and the ability to interact with others. In this sense, if someone is in a permanently unconscious state, one might consider that the "person" has died, even though the body is being maintained with machines. After centuries of believing that the heart was the "seat of life," scientists now know that it is not the heart but the brain that controls body functions, and most people believe that the brain is the seat of "person-hood." However, traditional attitudes change slowly. For example, many Japanese still believe that the heart is the seat of the soul and that death occurs when the heart stops. This has effectively banned transplant operations in Japan until now. When a heart transplant was performed there in 1968, the surgeon was accused of removing the heart from a live person, although the donor's brain was dead.

The new technology had made it clear that the definition of death needed to be changed. In 1968 a committee of experts at Harvard Medical School published a report that defined irreversible coma as the new criterion for death. Irreversible coma is described as total unawareness and unresponsiveness both to external stimulation and to inner needs, total absence of movement or spontaneous breathing, and absence of reflexes. Doctors can tell when the brain is completely dead by performing an electroencephalogram (EEG), or brain-wave recording. If the brain is not functioning, there is no electrical activity, and the recording will be "flat."

In 1981 the President's Commission for the Study of Ethical Problems in Medicine and Biomedical and Behavioral Research proposed the model Uniform Determination of Death Act, which defined death as irreversible cessation of circulatory and respiratory functions or irreversible cessation of all the functions of the entire brain. By 1988, taking their lead from the reports of these experts, more than forty states had changed their legal standard of death to include brain death. In Japan as well the idea of brain death is slowly gaining more acceptance, and the Japan Medical Society finally approved the new definition in 1988. This decision means that Japanese doctors should now be able to perform organ transplant operations.

The new era of technology has created knotty ethical dilemmas and agonizing choices. In 1976, the landmark case of Karen Ann Quinlan focused attention on the issues involved in the process of dying. For a year, twenty-one-year-old Karen had been in an irreversible coma, the apparent result of her using a combination of alcohol and tranquilizers. She was being kept alive on a respirator, and her doctors were certain she would never wake up; assisted by machines, however, she might live for years. After much agonizing over their decision, her parents asked the doctors to turn off the machines, but the doctors refused. The Quinlans then petitioned to have all "extraordinary procedures" discontinued, but the lower court turned them down. Finally, the New Jersey Supreme Court reversed the lower court's decision and granted the request in 1976. The judicial opinion was based on the constitutional right of an individual to privacy. It noted that although the state has a duty to preserve life, there comes a point at which a person's right to privacy and to refusal of bodily invasion overcomes the state's interest. The court stated that if Karen's guardian, family, attending physicians, and hospital ethics committee all agreed that there was no hope of recovery and that life support systems should be discontinued, then the support could be withdrawn without any civil or criminal liability. In other words, the judge decided that nature should take its course and that Karen Quinlan had a right to die.

Ironically, after Karen's respirator was disconnected, she lived for nine more years, sustained by tube feeding. But the controversy lives on.

Many people have questioned the morality of "pulling the plug." If that act results in death, is it the same as killing the patient? Some people think so. In 1983, two California doctors were charged with murder after they honored the family's request to disconnect Clarence Herbert's respirator and intravenous feeding tubes. Herbert had undergone cancer surgery, and in the recovery room his heart stopped. He was resuscitated, but his brain had been so severely damaged that he was left in a permanent vegetative state. Knowing there was no chance he would recover, Herbert's family and doctors agreed to remove his life support systems. He died within several days. The state brought criminal charges against the doctors, but eventually the California Court of Appeals dismissed the charges. The court said that a physician has no duty to continue treatment that has been proven ineffective. It also stated that the patient has a right to refuse medical treatment. In Herbert's case, since he was not competent to decide for himself, his wife was the surrogate decision-maker.

This was the first case in which doctors were charged with a criminal act for withdrawing life supports. The final court ruling was important because it underlined the philosophy that these decisions should be made by the patient, family, and doctor. The court made another significant decision, in finding that tube feeding was no different from a life support system such as a respirator. This was the first time an appeals court had approved the withdrawal of a feeding tube.

About 5,500 people die in the United States every day, and it is estimated that several hundred of them, like Clarence Herbert, die after life support systems have been disconnected. But as did not happen in Herbert's case, most of these decisions are made by informal, mutual agreement of family, patient, and doctors. For example, people whose kidneys have failed often make the decision to stop dialysis, knowing they will die but choosing to end their suffering. According to one study, about 20 percent of long-term dialysis patients decide to stop their treatment. Because most people these days do not die suddenly, there is often time to make plans about treatment. One newly widowed woman remarked that it was much easier when God made the decisions. As New Jersey judge Marie Garibaldi wrote, "questions of fate have become questions of choice."

Doctors and hospitals have been fearful of being sued or prosecuted for causing a patient's death. There has also been much confusion and disagreement about the ethics of medical decisions that may result in death. Some hospitals have used devious practices to avoid legal problems. Physicians at one New York hospital, for instance, stuck purple dots on the charts of patients who were terminally ill or irreversibly comatose, as a sign that they were not to be resuscitated if they had a cardiac arrest or stopped breathing. Doctors at another hospital wrote "do not resuscitate," or DNR, orders on a blackboard and erased them after the patients died. Many hospitals used a "slow code," which means that the resuscitation team acts so slowly that their efforts fail. These tactics have been used because of the lack of guidelines.

People who are comatose and who cannot make decisions for themselves must be protected. Sometimes families disagree among themselves about what kind of treatment a permanently comatose relative would have wanted. The lower courts often make the "safe" decision, endorsing the principle that life must be preserved at all costs. However, these judicial opinions are frequently overturned by appeals courts, as in the Quinlan case.

The way people think about death has been changing. A generation ago, most people were opposed to "pulling the plug." By contrast, in 1986, 90 percent of the 2,000 Americans polled in one survey believed strongly that adults who are competent to make their own decisions should have the right to refuse treatment. Another 1986 survey revealed that

73 percent of the persons polled approved of "withdrawing life support systems, including food and water, from hopelessly ill or irreversibly comatose patients if they or their family request it."

On both the national and the local level, a number of organizations work to provide information and foster public discussion of legal and moral issues such as the care of people who are terminally ill and the right to refuse treatment. In addition, groups such as the Society for the Right to Die encourage people to make out a document known as a "living will." This states that you do not want your life prolonged with useless medical procedures or machines if your condition is hopeless. It gives people the opportunity to express their wishes in advance, and to specify what they want in the way of treatment. For instance, if you should be in a permanently unconscious condition, you may not want mechanical respiration if your breathing ceases. But you might not want anyone to stop giving you food and water. You may also designate someone to make decisions for you when you are unable to do so. Thirty-eight states and the District of Columbia had passed living-will or right-to-die legislation as of late 1988, and court decisions in other states have upheld the patient's right to refuse treatment, even if it results in death. Each state has its own living-will form to be used by its residents. If you live in a state that does not have such a law, you can still make out a document that expresses your wishes, although your will may not be legally recognized in your state. Perhaps it sounds too unpleasant to dwell on the thought of dying, but making a decision about how you want to be treated is at least as important as deciding who inherits your money.

The following is an example of a Living Will as presented in Title 18, Section 5253 of the Vermont Statutes Annotated.

Vermont

LIVING WILL
(Terminal Care Document)

To my family, my physician, my lawyer, my clergyman. To any medical facility in whose care I happen to be. To any individual who may become responsible for my health, welfare or affairs.

Death is as much a reality as birth, growth, maturity and old age—it is the one certainty of life. If the time comes when I, _____, can no longer take part in decisions of my future, let this statement stand as an expression of my wishes, while I am still of sound mind.

If the situation should arise in which I am in a terminal state and there is no reasonable expectation of my recovery, I direct that I be allowed to die a natural death and that my life not be prolonged by extraordinary measures. I do, however, ask that medication be mercifully administered to me to alleviate suffering even though this may shorten my remaining life.

This statement is made after careful consideration and is in accordance with my strong convictions and beliefs. I want the wishes and directions here expressed carried out to the extent permitted by law. Insofar as they are not legally enforceable, I hope that those to whom this Will is addressed will regard themselves as morally bound by these provisions.

Signed: _____ Date: _____

Witness: _____ Witness: _____

Copies of this request have been given to:

_____

_____

_____

_____

Physicians traditionally have been committed to the preservation of life and the relief of suffering, but sometimes one duty conflicts with the other. The authors of an article published in *The New England Journal of Medicine* comment that "technology competes with compassion." Some physicians believe that their primary commitment is to use every possible means to prolong a person's life, no matter how hopeless the prognosis. But medical opinion as well as public opinion has been changing.

In March 1986, the Council on Ethical and Judicial Affairs of the American Medical Association issued a statement concerning withholding or withdrawing life-prolonging medical treatment. According to the Council, the choice should be left to the patient, or to the family or legal guardian if the patient is not competent to decide. In the fall of 1987, the Hastings Center, an institution devoted to the study of medical ethics, published similar guidelines after experts in law, medicine, and health care spent two and a half years researching and discussing the problem. The Hastings researchers also affirmed the right of the individual to refuse any life-sustaining treatment. They recommended that all health care institutions develop written policies concerning such matters as stopping treatment, performing cardiopulmonary resuscitation (CPR), and tube feeding. At the same time, in 1987 New York became the first state to pass a law requiring hospitals, nursing homes, and mental institutions to withhold emergency resuscitation from patients who have decided in advance that they do not want CPR, even if they are not terminally ill. As of January 1988, all hospitals were required by the Joint Commission on Accreditation of Healthcare Organizations to develop so-called DNR ("do not resuscitate") policies as a requirement for accreditation.

The use of CPR over the past twenty-five years has been

commonplace, and is standard medical procedure whenever someone's breathing or heartbeat stops. Take the case of Ken, a healthy ten-year-old boy who fell through the ice while skating. He was unconscious and not breathing when the rescue squad pulled him from the water twenty minutes later, but they gave him artificial respiration and rushed him to the hospital. Without CPR he would have died; instead he recovered completely. Everyone would agree that the rescue squad made the correct decision.

Compare Ken's case with that of forty-one-year-old Peter Cinque, a diabetic who was blind, had severe kidney damage, and had undergone partial amputation of both legs, because of complications from his diabetes. He needed kidney dialysis three times a week. He also was suffering from a bleeding ulcer and was in great pain, but his mind was alert. Peter discussed his situation with his family and with a Catholic priest. He then announced that he wanted to discontinue the dialysis and die in peace, at home. Two psychiatrists examined him and found him perfectly clear and competent to make a decision about treatment. The hospital, however, continued to treat him and obtained a court order to do so. A few days later, Peter suddenly stopped breathing; the doctors placed him on a respirator and saved his life. But by that time he was in an irreversible coma and probably had only six months to live, even with treatment. The court finally granted the wishes of Peter, his family, and the appointed guardian, and ordered the hospital to discontinue all treatment. Treatment was discontinued immediately, and Peter died before his family arrived at the hospital.

Can you see a difference between these two cases? Is it always appropriate to revive someone who has stopped breathing? Do you think the doctors should have resuscitated Peter after he stopped breathing? Is it ethical to keep someone alive against his or her wishes, despite the fact that it would cause unnecessary suffering?

American law supports the premise that people who are mentally competent can refuse any kind of treatment, even if refusing would be detrimental. Some people refuse treatment for personal reasons, while others, such as Christian Scientists and Jehovah's Witnesses, refuse because of religious convictions.

There have been numerous cases involving Jehovah's Witnesses, who do not allow blood transfusions because of the biblical injunction against eating blood. To them, receiving someone else's blood is the same as eating it. The law and the courts have upheld their rights to self-determination, with some exceptions. For example, parents cannot refuse transfusions for their minor children. Blood may be given, as well, if there is a life-threatening emergency requiring immediate transfusion.

An especially thorny problem may arise if a pregnant Jehovah's Witness refuses a needed transfusion, thereby placing her baby's life in jeopardy. Some think that the woman should be coerced to accept treatment for the sake of the "second patient," namely, the fetus. They think that a fetus should always be considered in the same category as minor children. Others believe that a woman should have total control over her own body. What would you decide in a case like this? Would the stage of pregnancy have any bearing on your decision? Hospital ethics committees must wrestle with these problems and formulate ethical guidelines. It took one such committee over two years to reach agreement about policies regarding the treatment of Jehovah's Witnesses.

The AIDS epidemic has provoked more discussion about making choices in advance. One doctor was quoted in *The*

New York Times as saying that AIDS "telescopes what we will all go through. . . . Most of us will die of a chronic, progressive disease that will be painful to watch, expensive, and ultimately fatal." Tom Wirth was a New Yorker who had seen many friends die a slow, agonizing death from AIDS. In order to avoid the same fate, he made out a living will, expressing his wishes not to be treated with extraordinary measures, and he designated a friend to act as proxy if he became incapacitated. Wirth became ill with AIDS and eventually was hospitalized, comatose with a brain infection. Despite his prior instructions, and over the objections of his friend, doctors insisted on treating his infection. The court sided with the doctors, and treatment was continued. Despite the treatment, Wirth died shortly thereafter. If New York State had had a living-will statute, his wishes probably would have been honored. Another problem in the case was that New York State law did not recognize a proxy. In addition, the term "extraordinary measures" was too vague, and there was disagreement as to what it meant. Indeed, what was extraordinary ten years ago is ordinary medical treatment today.

Daniel Callahan, director of the Hastings Center and an expert in the field of bioethics, stirred up some hot debate when he expressed his opinion that society cannot keep striving to extend old age and fend off death. He opposes mercy killing but thinks we should recognize a reasonable life span beyond which there would be a cutoff point for aggressive lifesaving treatment. Because of the enormous costs of health care, Callahan believes the United States needs a better way of allocating the available resources. He would spend more money to improve the quality of life for elderly people, on better nursing home care for instance, and to find ways of preventing or treating the diseases that strike in old age. Opponents object to the idea of using an arbitrary age limit and to limiting treatment on the basis of cost. On the other hand, Callahan believes that most people do not want their lives extended when life is no longer worth living for them.

To counter the case for pulling the plug, consider the story of Jacqueline Cole, which, her husband said, "muddied the waters" concerning the right to die. At forty-three she had a brain hemorrhage and fell into a coma, and then suffered a heart attack, a collapsed lung, and a blood infection. She had earlier asked her family to terminate life support if she ever became hopelessly ill. A court turned down her husband's request to stop treatment after she had been comatose for forty-one days. Six days later Mrs. Cole woke up. According to one neurologist, it was probably too soon to predict the outcome at the time Mr. Cole made his request.

Another controversy involves tube feeding. According to the American Medical Association, there are about 10,000 people in the United States who are in permanently unconscious condition and are maintained by tube feedings. Paul Brophy was one of these people. He was a forty-five-year-old fireman and emergency medical technician who lapsed into an irreversible coma after suffering a brain hemorrhage in 1983. As a member of his hometown rescue squad, he had responded to many accident calls, and he had often told family and friends that he would not want to be kept alive artificially. He spent a year in the hospital, during which he remained in a persistent vegetative state and needed to be fed through a gastrostomy tube (a tube inserted through the abdomen directly into the stomach). Knowing there was no hope of recovery, his wife asked the doctors to discontinue the feeding. The hospital refused, and a lower court agreed, even though the judge took note of the fact that Brophy would have wanted the tube removed. Finally, in 1986, the state supreme court reversed the earlier decision. The trial aroused some bitter debate. Opponents, including three dissenting justices, said that removing the tube would be tantamount to suicide or mercy killing. However, the court ruled that the cause of death would be the underlying condition that prevented Brophy from swallowing, not removal of the tube. Paul Brophy did not want to die, but he did not want to live in a vegetative state. The court also said that a feeding tube that a patient does not want is intrusive and can be considered extraordinary treatment. Although one dissenting judge said that withholding food and water would result in a gruesome death by starvation and dehydration, the majority agreed with the medical experts who testified that people in permanently unconscious states do not suffer pain. Paul Brophy died peacefully of pneumonia about a week after his tube feedings were discontinued.

Many people are concerned about the growing tendency to consider food and water as extraordinary treatment in certain situations. Some theologians and right-to-life organizations believe that food and water are basic human needs that should never be removed.

According to Catholic tradition, life is not an absolute value, and it need not be prolonged at all costs. In 1957, Pope Pius XII stated that people have the right and duty to take necessary treatment to preserve life and health, but that one is not obliged to use means that involve too grave a burden. Therefore, when the treatment becomes too burdensome and has little chance of success, there is no moral obligation to continue. The parents of Karen Quinlan, practicing Catholics, made their decision in light of this philosophy. They, however, did not request that Karen's feeding tube be removed. Some Catholics, along with many others, believe that artificial feeding is a treatment like kidney dialysis and respirators, and so can be discontinued under appropriate circumstances. The Catholic Church is divided on this issue.

Some people fear that the distinction between allowing someone to die naturally and mercy killing will disappear. In other words, if a doctor can allow someone to starve to death, it might be permissible to curtail suffering even more by administering a painless overdose. This is called the "slippery slope" argument by those who believe that our society will slide further down toward eliminating not only hopelessly ill people but also the handicapped, the retarded, and others who might be regarded as useless. They fear that acceptance of mercy killing might lead to the same atrocities that Nazi doctors perpetrated. Other experts disagree with this argument. They point out that the Nazis did not have any compassionate motivation or concern for people's rights, and that there is no parallel.

Although the word *euthanasia* means simply "good death," most people associate it with mercy killing. James Rachels, a philosophy professor and author of the book *The End of Life*, makes the distinction between allowing someone to die (passive euthanasia) and intentionally killing (active euthanasia). While there is widespread acceptance of the right-to-die concept among physicians, most reject the idea of actively taking a patient's life or assisting in a suicide. Yet there is an increasing movement toward active euthanasia.

A 1987 poll in California revealed that 64 percent of the people questioned were in favor of active euthanasia for hopelessly ill patients. The Hemlock Society and other organizations have sought to promote the rights of terminally ill people to end their lives, and have supported legislation that would permit them to request help from physicians. The

Hemlock Society does not condone suicide for any reasons other than that of terminal illness, and it emphasizes the point that it should be a personal decision. In 1988 a referendum was proposed in California that would have allowed physicians to comply with a terminally ill patient's request for a lethal injection. The Roman Catholic Church of America and the California Medical Association opposed it, but many physicians who have treated terminally ill patients favor this kind of legislation, provided there are strict controls. Among the potential abuses are the possibility of coercion from family members, difficulties in determining if the patient is capable of making an informed decision, and the chance of mistaken diagnosis.

One Kansas physician predicts that an increasing number of elderly people will seek "rational suicide" in the near future, and that doctors need to clarify their own thinking about how to deal with the problem. Some physicians have admitted to assisting actively the death of terminal patients who were in great pain. Many years after the fact, it was revealed that Lord Dawson, the royal physician, used morphine and cocaine to hasten the death of King George V of England.

A sizable number of people in the Netherlands favor active, voluntary euthanasia, which is said to account for 1,000 to 7,000 deaths a year, even though it is classified as murder. However, under strict criteria developed by Dutch courts, doctors are almost never prosecuted, and those convicted have received lenient sentences. The guidelines require that the request come from the patient, not a relative or anyone else; the patient must be capable of making a rational decision; his or her suffering must be unbearable; the physician must have a long-term relationship with the patient; and the request must be made repeatedly over a period of time. Not all Dutch physicians agree that active euthanasia should be lawful, but in Holland its practice is more widespread and the debate more open than in the United States and most other countries.

Jim was a young man who was dying from a malignant tumor. The doctors operated to remove the original growth from his abdomen, but the cancer had already spread throughout his body. Jim was in constant pain, even though he received injections of a powerful painkiller every four hours. During the day the pain was not so bad, but at night it became worse, and the effects of the injection lasted only an hour or so. It was so agonizing that he could not help moaning and crying out until the next shot gave him some relief. Even when the dose of medication was increased, he was never free of the excruciating pain. Jim knew he was terminally ill and had only a short time to live, but he did not want to continue living in constant agony. He asked his doctor to give him a large enough dose of the painkiller for him to die peacefully. If you were Jim's doctor, would you have considered giving him a lethal injection? Do you think assisted suicide can be condoned under some circumstances, or is it always wrong?

There have been numerous court cases involving people who could not bear to watch their loved ones suffering during a terminal illness. In 1985 Roswell Gilbert killed his wife of forty years, at her request. She was suffering from Alzheimer's disease, a progressive deterioration of the brain which leads to memory loss, confusion, inability to perform even simple tasks or self-care, loss of control over bodily functions, and finally death. A Florida court found him guilty of first-degree murder and sent him to prison. Other courts have dealt more leniently with mercy killers.

In April of 1989, Rudy Linares entered the hospital room

of his comatose and irreversibly brain-damaged sixteen-month-old son, and unplugged the baby's life support system. He cradled the child in his arms and wept as he kept hospital workers away with a gun. When the baby was dead, Linares surrendered. He said he did it out of love for his son, presumably in desperation, since some months earlier, the family had requested that life-support systems be withdrawn, but the doctor had refused, fearing he would be prosecuted. Many family members and friends supported his action; others sympathized but condemned his behavior as wrong. Linares was charged with first-degree murder, but the charges were later dropped.

There has been a significant increase in the number of reported mercy killings in the 1980s, and there are undoubtedly many more that have not been acknowledged officially. Some experts think the laws should be changed to include the category of mercy killing, so that courts can deal more fairly and realistically with this issue.

Many cultures have accepted mercy killings. As mentioned earlier, the Greeks in ancient Athens and Sparta approved the killing of defective newborn babies. They did not generally approve of suicide but believed it was appropriate under some circumstances, such as in cases of incurable disease or suffering. They did not make any significant distinction between suicide and assisted death. According to James Rachels, the Greek physician Hippocrates, who is known as the father of medicine, was in the minority in respect to his view about euthanasia; the Hippocratic Oath contains a pledge that prohibits physicians from assisting suicide. The Romans considered life to have no value unless it was meaningful and happy, and they accepted suicide in some situations. In contrast, the early Christians believed that killing was almost always wrong. Jewish and Islamic law as well as

Christian law forbid active euthanasia. Most Eastern re-
ligions, such as Confucianism, Shintoism, and Buddhism,
accept suicide under some circumstances.

In the sixteenth century, the English philosopher and
statesman Sir Thomas More wrote that people should choose
to die if they are in lingering pain from a hopeless disease.
According to Rachels, this was the first major evidence of a
change in Western thinking about euthanasia. Subsequently,
more theologians and philosophers gradually began to reject
the rigid views of earlier times.

In the present time, the process of dying is no longer as
simple as it was. The choices and issues are more complicated, and they often give rise to seemingly insoluble dilemmas. Should an individual be kept alive by all possible
means, no matter how hopeless the situation, or how painful
and debilitating the disease? Should a physician prolong the
life of an infant born without most of his brain or should the
baby be allowed to die peacefully without the use of the
latest medical technology available? Is there a real difference
between disconnecting a respirator and pulling out a feeding
tube? If a patient refuses life-saving treatment, is that the
same as committing suicide? Is it ethical to perform experiments on animals in order to benefit humans? Will genetic
research lead to the frightening possibility of scientists creating monsters?

If you were the person involved in any of the cases described in this book, what outcome would you want for your-
self? You probably have formed some opinions about the
issues raised here. Who is really qualified to answer these
questions? Many experts, including theologians, philosophers, ethicists, judges, legal scholars, scientists, treating
physicians and other health care professionals, hospital ethics committees, and groups of concerned lay people are help-

ing to clarify the complicated dilemmas spawned by modern technology.

But there are no simple answers, and it is important for every individual to make his or her own personal choices, about death as well as about life.

Suggestions for Further Reading

Altman, Lawrence K., *Who Goes First? The Story of Self-Experimentation in Medicine.* New York: Random House, 1987.

Bender, David L., and Bruno Leone, eds. *Biomedical Ethics: Opposing Viewpoints.* St. Paul, MN: Greenhaven Press, 1987.

Callahan, Daniel, *Setting Limits: Medical Care in an Aging Society.* New York: Simon and Schuster, 1987.

Colen, B. D., *Hard Choices: Mixed Blessings of Modern Technology.* New York: G. P. Putnam's Sons, 1986.

Dolan, Edward F., *Animal Rights.* New York: Franklin Watts, 1986.

Heintze, Carl, *Medical Ethics.* New York: Franklin Watts, 1987.

Hyde, Margaret O., and Elizabeth Forsyth, *AIDS: What Does It Mean to You?* (3rd edition). New York: Walker, 1990.

Hyde, Margaret O., and Lawrence E. Hyde, *Cloning and the New Genetics.* Hillside, NJ: Enslow, 1984.

Hyde, Margaret O., and Lawrence E. Hyde, *Meeting Death.* New York: Walker, 1989.

Levine, Howard, *Life Choices.* New York: Simon and Schuster, 1986.

Macklin, Ruth, *Mortal Choices.* New York: Pantheon, 1987.

Newton, David E., *Science Ethics.* New York: Franklin Watts, 1987.

Rachels, James, *The End of Life.* New York: Oxford University Press, 1986.

Scully, Thomas and Celia, *Playing God: The New World of Medical Choices.* New York: Simon and Schuster, 1987.

Stephens, Martin L., *Alternatives to Current Uses of Animals in Research, Safety Testing, and Education: A Layman's Guide.* Washington, DC: The Humane Society of the United States, 1986.

Weiss, Ann E., *Bioethics: Dilemma in Modern Medicine.* Hillside, NJ: Enslow, 1985.

Index

174
Hyd   Hyde, Margaret O.
           Medical dilemmas

DATE DUE			
NOV 24			
MAY 5			
FEB 13			
APR 15			
NOV. 18			
3/14/03			

152   91